THE BRITISH MUSEUM

VISITOR'S GUIDE

15 Self-Guided Tours

John Reeve

Thanks and Acknowledgements

First to Carla Turchini for her elegant design and extraordinary patience, and to Nina Shandloff for her editorial support. In Education I must thank Norman Divall for all his work not only on the many versions of the text, but in chasing images and data; to Richard Woff, Sam Moorhead and Kim Lawson for reading the text, and commenting on it, and in Kim's case walking the Museum with it. Finally, thanks to colleagues too numerous to mention who checked text and found images, and to the Photographic Service for producing them.
JFR

Silver drinking horn (rhyton) from Turkey, 5th–4th century BC. A fine example of the art of the Achaemenid empire, which dominated the ancient Near East from the age of Cyrus and Darius in 6th-century BC Iran and beyond until Alexander the Great conquered in 334 BC. (**52**)

previous page
The Buddhist goddess Tara, gilded bronze, from Sri Lanka, 8th century AD. (**33**)

opposite page
Head of Christ from the Hinton St Mary mosaic, Roman Britain, 4th century AD, the earliest securely dated head of Christ. (**49**)

Front cover illustrations *(top to bottom)*: details of the ancient Egyptian figure of Katep; Buddhist sculpture from India; ancient Greek vase painting by Exekias.

© 2003 The Trustees of the British Museum

First published in 2003 by The British Museum Press
A division of The British Museum Company Ltd
38 Russell Square, London WC1B 3QQ
www.britishmuseum.co.uk

Reprinted 2003, 2004 (three times), 2005, 2006 (twice)

ISBN-13: 978-0-7141-2780-4
ISBN-10: 0-7141-2780-9

A catalogue record for this book is available from the British Library

Photography by the British Museum Department of Photography and Imaging; additional photographs by Nigel Young (Foster and Partners) and Phil Sayer
Maps by Jeffery Design Ltd, Nigel Coath and Turchini Design Ltd
Designed and typeset in Bliss by Turchini Design Ltd
Printed and bound in Belgium by Proost NV

Contents

How to use this tour guide

There is no right way to visit the British Museum – it's up to you, and how much time and energy you have.

If this is your first visit then take Tour 1, and after that see whether you want to know more about the ancient world (Tour 2), or other parts of the Museum (Tours 3, 4 or 5).

If you know the Museum already, start with one of Tours 2–5, or take a thematic tour (Animals, Jewellery, Money, Pottery, Sculpture, Seven Wonders, Time, Writing). Two new galleries (Enlightenment, and Living and dying) are also featured (pp.78–81).

If you have children with you, you might start with Tour 1, and then use the family audio tour with Stephen Fry (see opposite) or take a back pack or family trail.

You can return to the Great Court at any time for coffee, lunch or tea. You might combine a tour with self-guiding yourself using this guide.

Note that numbers in bold refer to gallery numbers.

Other tours of the Museum

Highlights tours by professional tourist guides will introduce you to some of the major ancient cultures. Enquire and book at the Information Desk in the Great Court.

EyeOpener tours by specially trained volunteer guides introduce individual galleries or specific areas of the collection, 10 times or more a day. Meet in the gallery: details in a special leaflet and in 'What's on', available from the Information Desk and Box Office.

Gallery talks by curators and educators, and other events, are also listed in the free 'What's on' leaflet.

Or take an audio tour:

Highlights audio tour
Short commentaries on some of the most important star objects and less well-known artefacts from the Museum's collection. Available in English and Spanish from the Information Desk.

Family audio tour
Join Stephen Fry on a trail of bodies, beasts and board games.

Enlightenment Gallery audio tour
Neil MacGregor, Director of the British Museum, is your guide to the permanent exhibition called Enlightenment: Discovering the World in the 18th Century (**1**), displayed in the magnificently restored room formerly known as the King's Library.

Parthenon audio tour
In-depth commentaries on the Parthenon sculptures by curator Ian Jenkins. Available in seven languages from the Parthenon galleries (**18**).

And use the Reading Room:

To find out more about objects that you see or the cultures from which they come, use the **Paul Hamlyn Library** in the round Reading Room, and the **COMPASS** database also available there, and online at www.thebritishmuseum.ac.uk/compass.

The Reading Room (1854–7) in which Karl Marx wrote *Das Kapital* and which is now open to all visitors for the first time as an information centre. The upper storeys house part of the anthropology library.

Welcome to the British Museum

The British Museum is one of the world's most visited museums and covers an astonishing range of cultures, periods and types of material. Unlike the Louvre or the Hermitage it is not based on a royal collection in a former royal palace; unlike either of those museums or the Metropolitan Museum in New York it doesn't collect Western oil paintings. It does, however, collect graphic art (prints, drawings and watercolours) from both East and West, as well as paintings from Asia.

The Museum today reflects many moments of its past history. From its foundation in 1753 as the oldest national, public and secular museum anywhere, it presents the Age of Enlightenment and Discovery in the Enlightenment Gallery (**1**) in the restored former King's Library, the oldest part of the Greek Revival building that from the 1820s replaced the converted aristocratic mansion in which the Museum first opened in 1759.

Ugandan pots (19th–20th century) made for the Baganda king's palace. (**25**)

The 18th- and early 19th-century passion for the classical is reflected in the number of Greek and Roman galleries on three floors and their extensive coverage of the Mediterranean world and its neighbours (**11–23**; **69–73**; **77–85**). The 19th-century interest in ancient Egypt and the Bible lands is evident in the collections of what are now the Departments of Ancient Egypt and the Sudan (**4**, **61–66**) and the Ancient Near East (**6–10**, **51–59**, **88–89**). Asian cultures have

Sir Hans Sloane (1660–1753), doctor, naturalist and founding father of the British Museum. He was an avid collector of natural history, books and everything from Chinese art to North American ethnography. The breadth of his interests and collecting decisively influenced the Museum. As an Enlightenment polymath, his world is explored in the Enlightenment Gallery (**1**) where his bust by Rysbrack can be seen. His aim was 'satisfying the desire of the curious, as for the improvement, knowledge and information of all persons.'

Lycurgus Cup, Roman
glass, 4th century AD. (41)

been an interest since the beginning, and as a result the British
Museum has one of the Western world's most comprehensive
collections from China, Japan, Korea, South Asia (particularly India) and
South-East Asia (**33a** and **b**, **34**, **67**, **91**, **92–4**).

This curiosity about the whole world and the urge to collect and
understand it is at the core of the ethnographic collections. These are
included in galleries for Africa (**25**), North America (**26**), Mexico (**27**)
and the Wellcome Trust Gallery (**24**) on living, dying and well-being in
world cultures. This is the current public face of a collection that
embraces material brought back from Captain Cook's voyages to the
Pacific in the 1770s *(see the Enlightenment Gallery, 1)*, textiles from all
over the world including tents, contemporary Aboriginal Australian art,
boats, a rice barn from Indonesia constructed inside the Museum, and
papier-mâché skeletons from Mexico for the 'Day of the Dead' festival.
Fieldwork in recent years has contributed to collections from Central
Asia, Papua New Guinea, Bolivia, Eastern Europe, the Nicobar Islands
and Madagascar, to name only a few.

In another thematic collection, the Coins and Medals Department
presents money of all kinds from around the world in **68** *(see p.56)* as
well as art medals (some are on show in **46** and **47**) and modern
badges. Money is also displayed in temporary exhibitions in **69a** and
in galleries such as Asia (**33**).

'Yarla Jukurrpa (Bush Potato Dreaming)', by
Victor Jupurrula Ross of Yuendumu, Northern
Territory, Australia. Acrylic paint on canvas,
1986. © Victor Jupurrula Ross/DACS 2003

The original universal ambition of the Museum to embrace all knowledge in the arts and sciences is depicted on the pediment above the main entrance. This ambition, now shared with other national museums and galleries in Britain, was partly realised in this building, at least for a time: the natural history collections left in the 1880s, after more than a century; the British Library departed finally in 1998. The national collections of painting and portraits are in the National Gallery, Tate and the National Portrait Gallery; the Victoria & Albert and Design Museums have taken on the leading role in inspiring, collecting and displaying design. The Victoria & Albert Museum and British Library also collect Asian and Islamic art, as does the British Museum. Many major museums and galleries in Britain collect British art and archaeology, but this Museum has the national collections of British archaeology and of prints and drawings, including much British art, notably by Blake and Turner. Prints, drawings and watercolours ranging from Leonardo da Vinci to Pablo Picasso are shown regularly in temporary exhibitions.

The history and archaeology of Britain are seen in a wider world

left
Leonardo da Vinci (1452–1519), 'Bust of a Warrior in Profile', metal point on cream-coloured prepared paper. In the style of his master Verrocchio whose studio he entered c.1470, this may represent the Persian king Darius.

right
Pablo Picasso (1881–1973), study for 'Les Demoiselles d' Avignon' of 1906–7, drawing in bodycolour and watercolour. © Succession Picasso/DACS 2003

and European context in the Upper floor galleries (**36–50**) from the age of Stonehenge to the present day. Through the Partnership UK scheme with museums such as Norwich, Manchester, Exeter and the Sutton Hoo Visitor Centre, the Museum's archaeological collections travel extensively and joint projects are developed. Museum archaeologists excavate in Britain and other parts of the world.

Today the Museum plays a significant role internationally, working with museums, collectors, archaeologists, researchers and artists from Japan and Korea to Mexico and Brazil. Its scope is unparalleled, and because of its continuity of collecting and research, so too is the depth of the evidence it offers for world cultures. The challenge is how to keep abreast of cultural change and new interpretations, and how to renew displays and facilities. The Great Court, the Museum's Millennium project at the heart of the Museum in space previously occupied by the Library, epitomises physically this process of renewal. It gives you the opportunity to choose how to construct your own Museum visit rather than forcing you through a particular route. The purpose of this guide is to help you do just that.

The Great Court, designed by Norman Foster as the Museum's Millennium Project. The facades of Smirke's 19th-century building have been restored (left), the round Reading Room is faced in stone and opened to all visitors for the first time (right), and an astonishing glass roof now covers the whole space. Sculpture includes the lion from Knidos (*see Animals tour, p.44*).

Tour 1
Introducing ancient civilisations

This short tour introduces some of the major ancient civilisations and a number of the British Museum's most famous exhibits.

The galleries on the Main floor were designed to house large pieces of sculpture from the ancient world. In the first century of the Museum's history, from the mid-18th to the mid-19th century, interest focused on ancient Greece and Rome, and then on ancient Egypt and the ancient Near East (especially what are now Iraq and Iran). You can explore these and other civilisations in greater depth in later tours.

From the Great Court go through the West door to the centre of the Egyptian sculpture gallery (4).

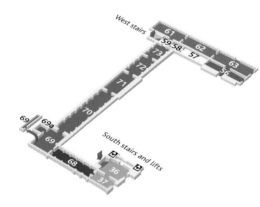

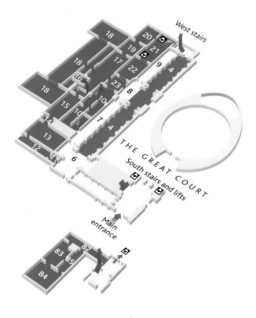

		Ur (c.2685 BC)		Stonehenge (c.2100 BC)	
	Egyptians (c.3200 BC)		Cycladic (c.3000 BC)		Minoans (c.2050 BC)
Sumerians (4000 BC) writing			Pyramids (c.2650 BC)		Babylon (1792 BC)
4000 BC			3000 BC		2000 BC

This gallery is arranged broadly chronologically after an introductory display featuring the Rosetta Stone, which was discovered by Napoleon's army at Rosetta in the Nile Delta. The same text on this slab is written in two Egyptian scripts and Greek; this enabled the meaning of Egyptian hieroglyphs finally to be deciphered. You will soon notice hieroglyphs on many other Egyptian exhibits such as the king list *(at the far left end)* and in the Upper floor galleries.

Several exhibits show the scale of Egyptian temples and sculpture: the giant fist, columns, and the massive torso of Ramesses II (c.1270 BC) in the distance. On a more intimate scale *(on the left-hand side)* is the sculpture of a husband and wife holding hands, with a detailed depiction of the wigs they are both wearing and their stiff linen clothes. Like all sculptures here (and most elsewhere in the Museum) this would have originally been painted.

Egyptian nobleman and his wife (c.1325 BC). (4)

opposite page
The Rosetta Stone (196 BC). (4)

below left
Head of Ramesses II (c.1270 BC). (4)

below right
Rahotpe seen with a table of offerings, from his tomb (c.2600 BC). (64)

Ramesses II (1270 BC)

Alexander the Great (336 BC)

Mycenae (1500 BC)

Assyrians (800 BC)

Rome (509 BC–410 AD)

Tutankhamun (1340 BC)   Solomon (966 BC)

Parthenon (447 BC)

1000 BC

BC/AD

Cycladic figurine (c.2800–2300 BC). (**11**)

Nereid, from the Nereid Monument (c.400 BC). (**17**)

*At this point, leave **4** and turn left to **17** (Greek and Roman).*

The development of Greek art over 1,500 years is traced in **11–16** down to the 5th century BC *(see Tour 2, p.16)*. In **17** is the reconstruction of the so-called Nereid Monument, from Xanthos in Lykia, south-west Turkey. The tomb of a local ruler, it is decorated with sculpture in the Greek style (c.390 BC) including the wind-swept Nereids, daughters of the sea god Nereus.

Ahead of you in **18** are the friezes, metopes and pedimental sculpture of the Parthenon, (5th century BC). They form one of the greatest surviving achievements of classical art, illustrating both myths and historical events. To your left and right idealised warriors on horseback follow a procession up on to the Acropolis in Athens. The climax comes immediately opposite you as a new robe is presented for the shrine to the goddess Athena. The seated gods (much larger in scale than the humans) look on. Notice *(to your right)* from one angle of the east pediment, the head of one of the tired horses that has pulled the chariot of the moon goddess Selene across the sky.

Later Greek art can be seen in **19–23**: 4th-century BC fragments from the Mausoleum at Halikarnassos, one of the

Parthenon sculptures (**18**):

above
Horse of Selene from the pediment (447–432 BC).

left
Horsemen from the frieze.

		Ur (c.2685 BC)		Stonehenge (c.2100 BC)	
	Egyptians (c.3200 BC)		Cycladic (c.3000 BC)		Minoans (c.2050 BC)
Sumerians (4000 BC) writing				Pyramids (c.2650 BC)	Babylon (1792 BC)
4000 BC		3000 BC		2000 BC	

Seven Wonders of the Ancient World, **21** *(see p.70)*; and Hellenistic art, **22**. Room **23** gives a glimpse of Roman art, marble versions of now lost Greek originals showing athletes with perfect physiques, and in the centre the 'Crouching Venus'. To see Roman art, take the stairs down from **23** to **82–85** *(Lower floor)*. Roman art is also on show upstairs in **70** and **49** *(see Tours 2 and 3)*.

Before you go on to the Egyptian mummies upstairs (see box on next page) you can briefly visit the Ancient Near East.

Facing you as you leave **22** and **23** are the figures of giant man-headed bulls, **10**, from an 8th-century BC Assyrian palace. In the 7th century BC the Assyrian empire, based in what is now Iraq, stretched from Egypt to Iran.

If you pass into **10** you will see the lionhunt reliefs from the walls of Ashurbanipal's palace at Nineveh (c.645 BC), with their graphic portrayal of stylised violence.

*Return to the Egyptian sculpture gallery, **4**, and then go to the far, northern end, up the West stairs, to see the Egyptian mummies **62–63**.*

left
Colossal figure from the Mausoleum at Halikarnassos (mid 4th-century BC). **(21)**

right
Dying lion from Assyrian frieze at Nineveh (c.645 BC). **(10)**

Ramesses II (1270 BC)		Alexander the Great (336 BC)
Mycenae (1500 BC)	Assyrians (800 BC)	Rome (509 BC–410 AD)
Tutankhamun (1340 BC)	Solomon (966 BC)	Parthenon (447 BC)
	1000 BC	BC/AD

Mummy case of
Artemidorus, 100–120 AD.
(**62**, *case 22*) from Roman
Egypt.

EGYPTIAN MUMMIES

Before mummification was invented, bodies
were dried out naturally in the desert (**64** – *see
p.20*). To ensure a successful afterlife for the
dead through mummification, most of their
internal organs – stomach, lungs, intestines,
liver – were removed and preserved in
distinctive jars (**63**, *case 6*). The brain
(although not the heart) was also removed, but
not preserved. The rest of the body was packed
with natural salt and tightly wrapped with
bandages. Small figures (shabtis) were also
buried to magically provide for the deceased.
A range of animals sacred to the gods – bulls,
crocodiles, cats and falcons – were also
mummified.

left and above right
The gilded inner coffin
of the priestess
Henutmehyt, 1250 BC
(**63**, *case 9*) (above right)
and her painted wooden
shabti box (left).

right
Mummy of a cat, after
30 BC. Cats were sacred
to the goddess Bastet.
(**62**)

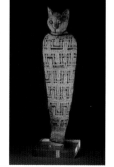

	Ur (c.2685 BC)		Stonehenge (c.2100 BC)	
Egyptians (c.3200 BC)		Cycladic (c.3000 BC)		Minoans (c.2050 BC)
Sumerians (4000 BC) writing			Pyramids (c.2650 BC)	Babylon (1792 BC)
4000 BC		3000 BC		2000 BC

Now either return to the Great Court via the bridge from **56**, or go via **61** (an introduction to Ancient Egypt) and cross the landing to **73–71** (Greek and Roman) and **70** (Rome).

The city of Rome was first occupied c.750 BC and began its epic expansion 400 years later. By 30 BC Rome had supplanted Greece politically, but Greek cultural influence remained strong. For more detail on these galleries see Tour 2 (p.18).

In the gallery of Rome, City and Empire, **70**, see the cameo-glass Portland Vase, a technical masterpiece and the most famous survival of a rare kind of object that is extremely

difficult to make. Badly damaged in the 19th century, it has been restored twice. Wedgwood's copy of it can be seen in **47**. The bronze head of Augustus is from the Sudan, at the limits of Roman influence.

An extraordinary outfit made from crocodile skin (case 18) comes from Egypt, land of Cleopatra.

Continue through **69** (Greek and Roman Daily Life), **68** (Money) and **36–37** (Prehistory), and return to the Weston Great Hall by the South stairs.

Bronze head of the Roman Emperor Augustus, c.27–25 BC, from Meroë, Sudan. (**70**)

left
The Portland Vase, 1st century BC–1st century AD, Roman cameo-glass. (**70**, case 12)

right
The Warren cup, c. 50–70 AD, Roman silver. Its Hellenised style and subject matter suggests that it comes from a Greek community in the eastern Mediterranean. (**70**, case 12a)

	Ramesses II (1270 BC)		Alexander the Great (336 BC)
Mycenae (1500 BC)		Assyrians (800 BC)	Rome (509 BC – 410 AD)
Tutankhamun (1340 BC)	Solomon (966 BC)		Parthenon (447 BC)
	1000 BC		BC/AD

Tour 2

Further into the ancient world

*From the Great Court, go through the West
door into Egyptian sculpture, 4, and then left;
at the far end turn right and enter the earliest
of the Greek galleries, 11.*

**Greek and Roman art,
*Rooms 11–23***

Art from the Cycladic Islands, **11**,
dates from a period (c.2500 BC)
when many great civilisations
such as Egypt, India and China
were developing. The pure,
stylised qualities of its figure
sculpture have attracted modern
artists such as Picasso, Moore,
Brancusi and Modigliani. The
ancient culture of another island,
Crete, **12**, includes exquisite
jewellery, powerfully decorated
pots and a bronze bull-leaper
(c.1600 BC) *(case 1)* linked with
the legends of King Minos and
the minotaur.

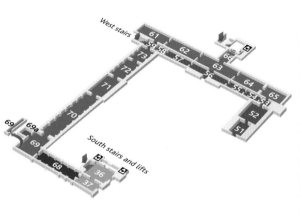

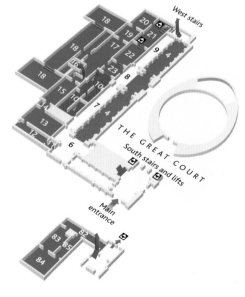

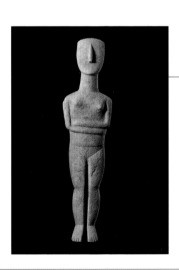

	Ur (c.2685 BC)		Stonehenge (c.2100 BC)	
Egyptians (c.3200 BC)		Cycladic (c.3000 BC)		Phoenicians (1700 BC)
Sumerians (4000 BC) writing			Pyramids (c.2650 BC) Mummification (c.2300 BC)	Babylon (1792 BC)
4000 BC		3000 BC		2000 BC

Following the chronological thread of galleries **13–15** you can see the development of sophisticated ceramics and their painted decoration showing scenes from myth, daily life, theatre and sport; and the emergence of naturalism in sculpting the human form. In addition to the Parthenon (**18**), other architectural and funerary sculpture from Athens can be seen in **19** (behind the Nereid Monument). The Hellenistic Gallery **22** brings us to the last climax of Greek culture – the age of Alexander the Great (356–323 BC). This reflects naturalism in sculpture such as the bronze head of Sophokles, and complex combinations of sculpture and architecture as in the column drum from Ephesos (Turkey), from one of the Seven Wonders of the Ancient World *(see p.71)*. By this date the influence of late Greek culture extended to southern France *(see Celtic Europe, 50)*, north-west India and Pakistan *(see Gandharan sculpture in South Asia, 33)*, Egypt, and southern Russia.

On the Upper floor you can see more Greek and Roman art in a geographical context.

Return to the Egyptian sculpture gallery, 4, left and up the stairs at the end, turn right at the top and explore Greek and Roman art further, starting in 73 (p.18). Alternatively, at this point you could go ahead to 59, Ancient Near East (p.19).

opposite page
Cycladic figurine
(c.2800–2300 BC). (**11**)

left
Minoan gold pendant
from the Aigina Treasure
(c.1750–1500 BC). (**12**)

right
Head of Sophokles,
Hellenistic period
(300–100 BC). (**22**)

Ramesses II (1270 BC)	Etruscans (c.850 BC)	First coins (620 BC)	Iran (c.550 BC)		Alexander the Great (336 BC)	
Mycenae (1500 BC)		Assyrians (800 BC)			Rome (509 BC – 410 AD)	
Tutankhamun (1340 BC)	Solomon (966 BC)	Homer (c.750 BC)	Hanging Gardens of Babylon (c.580 BC)	Battle of Marathon (490 BC)	Parthenon (447 BC)	
1000 BC			500 BC			BC/AD

ANCIENT GREECE AND ROME

Greek horse and rider from southern Italy (c.550 BC). (**73**)

In **73** (Greeks in Southern Italy) begin with a bronze horseman (*c.*500 BC) singled out by sculptor Henry Moore, and see also displays of characteristic Greek vases from this region. The mix of Greek and other cultures on Cyprus is shown in **72**, especially in the variety of stylised and naturalistic sculpture. In **71** you can see Etruscan and other cultures from Italy before the Roman empire, including, at the far end, the painted terracotta sarcophagus of a reclining woman, and a reconstruction of her head.

Continue through **70**, *Rome: City and Empire (see p.15), to* **69**, *Daily Life, or retrace your steps to* **59**.

Part of colossal statue from Cyprus (c.490–480 BC). (**72**)

Etruscan terracotta sarcophagus (c.150–130 BC). (**71**)

	Ur (c.2685 BC)		Stonehenge (c.2100 BC)	
	Egyptians (c.3200 BC)	Cycladic (c.3000 BC)		Phoenicians (1700 BC)
Sumerians (4000 BC) writing		Pyramids (c.2650 BC)	Mummification (c.2300 BC)	Babylon (1792 BC)
4000 BC		3000 BC		2000 BC

The Ancient Near East, *Rooms 59–54*

The lime plaster figures here on the landing, **59**, are some of the oldest large-scale sculptures of the human figure (c.7200 BC) and come from modern Jordan. The Museum excavates all over the world, and the next room, **58**, shows the contents of a kitchen from a Jordanian palace site found recently under later Egyptian period buildings. Many sites mentioned in the Bible are featured in **57**.

*Now go through **57** to Early Mesopotamia (modern Iraq), **56**. Here you see the development (from c.3100 BC) of the earliest writing on clay (case 3). See pp.74–5 for Writing tour.*

Spectacular discoveries in **56** from the Royal Tombs of Ur (c.2600 BC) include jewellery, lyres, the so-called 'Standard' and 'Royal Game', and the enigmatic figure of a goat. Later Mesopotamia (from c.1600 BC) continues in **55** with Babylonia on the left and Assyria on the right.

Material from Anatolia (modern Turkey) includes bronzes from Urartu (Ararat; c.700 BC) in **54**. Ancient Iran (**52**) includes Luristan bronzes (from c.1200 BC), the Cyrus cylinder and Persepolis and Susa reliefs (6th–5th century BC), the Oxus Treasure (5th–4th century BC) and Sasanian silver (3rd–7th century AD), from the period before Islam. Later Iranian art is in **34** (Islamic Art).

Babylonian cylinder of Nabonidus, with inscription mentioning Belshazzar (6th century BC). *(55, case 14)*

Figure of a goat from Ur (c.2600 BC). **(56)**

left
Gold armlet from the Oxus Treasure (5th–4th century BC). **(52)**

right
Royal Game of Ur (c.2600 BC). **(56)**

	Ramesses II (1270 BC)	Etruscans (c.850 BC)	First coins (620 BC) Iran (c.550 BC)	Alexander the Great (336 BC)
Mycenae (1500 BC)		Assyrians (800 BC)		Rome (509 BC – 410 AD)
Tutankhamun (1340 BC)	Solomon (966 BC)	Homer (c.750 BC) Hanging Gardens of Babylon (c.580 BC)	Battle of Marathon (490 BC) Parthenon (447 BC)	
1000 BC		500 BC		BC/AD

Ancient Egypt and the Sudan

*Return to the landing and go straight ahead through **65** into **64**, Early Egypt.*

By 12,000 BC Africans were forming settled communities in parts of the well-watered and fertile Sahara, and along the Nile. As the climate became drier, more people were forced into the Nile valley, kept fertile by annual floods. In the era before mummification and the first dynasties, bodies like the one dating from c.3250 BC (*case 15*) were dried out naturally in the desert.

This gallery also shows evidence of the earliest art and writing, technologies and religious rituals, and the beginning of monumental building with the earliest Pyramids (2600 BC).

Egypt became the greatest and most enduring of African kingdoms, despite periods of internal breakdown and foreign invasion. Egypt and Africa, **65**, traces the links between ancient Egypt and its neighbour to the south: both were conquered by the other. Nubia was the source of exotic imports including slaves and gold, seen in the painted cast on the wall (from the 13th century BC), brought as tribute to Ramesses II, builder of Abu Simbel.

The Nubian kingdom of Meroë remained independent long after Egypt became part of the Greek and Roman worlds.

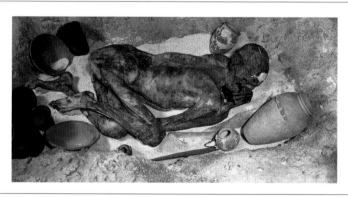

A naturally preserved ancient Egyptian body (c.3250 BC). (**64**)

opposite page, left Bronze cat representing the goddess Bastet, from Roman Egypt (after 30 BC). (**61**)

opposite page, right Painted cast of a relief of Ramesses II receiving tribute, from the temple of Beit el-wali, Nubia. (**65**)

	Ur (c.2685 BC)		Stonehenge (c.2100 BC)	
Egyptians (c.3200 BC)		Cycladic (c.3000 BC)		Phoenicians (1700 BC)
Sumerians (4000 BC) writing			Pyramids (c.2650 BC) Mummification (c.2300 BC)	Babylon (1792 BC)

4000 BC	3000 BC	2000 BC

See on the end wall a relief from a queen's tomb of the 2nd century BC. Early Christianity is revealed here *(case 17)* and in the Coptic Gallery, **66**. Islam reached Egypt and North Africa from the 600s AD: you can take the stairs or lift from beyond **66** to see mosque lamps and rock crystal from Islamic Egypt in **34** *(case 21)*.

You can also go on past the mummies in the Roxie Walker Galleries (**63–62**) to **61** for an introduction to many aspects of ancient Egypt, particularly decipherment, and examples of small-scale art such as the ear-ringed cat, one of many animals sacred to the ancient Egyptians. You can also find out about some of the Museum's current research projects in **61** *(closing late 2006)*.

You could follow a thematic tour such as Jewellery (p.48) or Pottery (p.58) after this overview.

Painting from the Theban tomb of Sobekhotep, c.1400 BC, showing Nubian tribute – gold, incense and animal skins. (**65**)

| Ramesses II (1270 BC) | Etruscans (c.850 BC) | First coins (620 BC) | Iran (c.550 BC) | | Alexander the Great (336 BC) |

Mycenae (1500 BC)   Assyrians (800 BC)   Rome (509 BC–410 AD)

Tutankhamun (1340 BC)   Solomon (966 BC)   Homer (c.750 BC)   Hanging Gardens of Babylon (c.580 BC)   Battle of Marathon (490 BC)   Parthenon (447 BC)

1000 BC   500 BC   BC/AD

Tour 3
Britain and Europe from prehistor

Go from the Great Court via the Weston Great Hall up the South stairs to **36**.

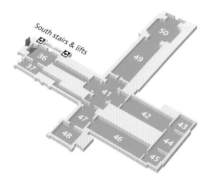

Rooms **49–50** (Celtic Europe; Roman Britain) reopen in early 2007. Until then a temporary display of some of the contents is on the Main Floor in Room **2**: enter from the Weston Great Hall via the Grenville Shop.

'Prehistory: Objects of Power' (**36**) introduces some of the key themes in interpreting evidence from the centuries before writing. Find the window that looks out over the Great Court below. *Case 1 is just behind you.* The display begins with the birth of technology and early stone tools from Olduvai in East Africa about 2 million years ago *(case 1)*. Even then objects had symbolic value – some are much too big to have been used easily *(see the hand-axe from Dorset (no.2) in case 1)*. Stone technology like this was in use until the introduction of metals about 8,000 years ago. Long before then art had appeared in the Ice Age with cave paintings and jewellery, and other objects carved from materials like ivory.

SEE ALSO

See prehistory also in:
● Greece (**11–12**)
● Asia (**33**)
● Ancient Near East (**59–57**)
● Ancient Egypt and Sudan (**64–65**)
● North America (**26**)

Farming (c.9000 BC)   Rice cultivation (Asia), first weaving (Near East) (c.6000 BC)

End of last ice age (c.10,000 BC)

Cave paintings (10,000 BC), earliest pots (Japan)   Domesticated animals (Near East) (c.7000 BC)

10,000 BC   5000 BC

o the present

The 12,500-year-old mammoth *(case 1)* is carved from reindeer antler and was part of a spear thrower from France. It expresses the close relationship between prehistoric people and the animals they depended on. From 12,000 years ago farming developed in Asia and the Ancient Near East, with harvesting of crops and domesticated animals. Surplus wealth from agriculture and trade encouraged the production of luxury goods like the gold cape from Mold in Flintshire, Wales *(case 4)*. This is an astonishing object dating from c.1900–1600 BC, and recently conserved for this new display. It clearly sent an unambiguous message about the status of the person wearing it.

The Rillaton gold cup (1700–1400 BC) from Cornwall *(case 7* in the far right-hand corner) is another stunning piece of Bronze Age technology, beaten from a single sheet of gold like the cape and with the handle attached by rivets. A gold collar from Portugal (900–700 BC) is by the door which leads through to **41**.

*Rooms **49–50** (Celtic Europe; Roman Britain) reopen in early 2007. Until then, some of the material discussed on pp.24–5 is on temporary display in Room **2**, on the Main Floor.*
*To continue with Early Medieval Europe, go straight ahead from **36** to **41**.*

opposite page
Mammoth carved from reindeer antler from France (c.10,500 BC). (**36**)

left
Gold cape from Mold, Wales (c.1900–1600 BC). (**2**)

	Glass (3000 BC)	Indus Valley (c.2500 BC)	Mold Cape (1900 BC)	
Sumerians (c.4000 BC)		Cycladic Greece, China, Egypt (c.3000 BC)		
	Wheel and plough, bronze (Near East), sail (Egypt) (c.3500 BC)		Stonehenge (c.2100 BC)	
4000 BC	3000 BC		2000 BC	1000 BC

Basse-Yutz flagon, France (c.400 BC).

Celtic Europe (*see note on p.22*)

Celtic culture ranged from Britain and France in the west across Europe to Romania in the east: elegant bronze wine flagons are from Basse-Yutz, in France (*c.*400 BC). Sensational discoveries have been made in recent years from Celtic Britain, notably Lindow Man, who was found in a Cheshire peat bog in 1984. He appears to have been the victim of a ritual killing: first stunned by a blow to the head, he was then garrotted, his throat was cut and he was pushed face down into a bog (which preserved his body). Many Celtic Iron Age objects have been found in rivers, including the Waterloo Helmet and the Battersea, Chertsey and Witham Shields. These were all deliberately placed in the rivers as offerings to the gods.

Bronze mirrors and golden torcs from eastern England show the sophistication and advanced technology of later Celtic Britain. At Welwyn Garden City (a short distance north of London) a burial included Mediterranean gaming pieces made of glass, Italian silver wine cups and wine storage jars (amphorae), the combination giving a good idea of what kind of afterlife was expected.

above
Battersea Shield
from River Thames
(1st century BC).

left
Bronze mirror from
Desborough, Northants
(1st century BC).

right
Lindow Man, Cheshire
(1st century BC).

Roman Republic (509 BC)   Parthenon (447 BC)

Iron Age (800–0 BC)   Etruscans (800–400 BC)

Maiden Castle hill fort (450 BC)

Roman Britain (*see note on p.22*)

Following a period of closer contact, the Romans invaded Britain in 43 AD. This collection reveals the interaction of two cultures over four centuries.

A model provides a reconstruction of life on the frontier of the empire: a Roman fort on Hadrian's Wall in northern Britain. In addition there are arms and armour as well as soldiers' tombstones. The Vindolanda tablets also reveal life in the Roman army. Images of several Roman emperors associated with Britain include Claudius, Nero and Hadrian. Treasures from Mildenhall and Hoxne, which combine pagan and Christian emblems, and from Thetford show the lavish lifestyle of the ruling class. There is evidence for early Christianity in the Water Newton Treasure – the earliest communion silver – and the wall paintings from a chapel at Lullingstone. The earliest securely dated head of Christ is found at the centre of a mosaic from Hinton St Mary, Dorset. The X and P are the first letters of Christ's name in Greek.

The burying of precious hoards such as those found at Thetford and Hoxne shows that there was massive disruption as the Roman empire disintegrated. The next group of galleries tell the story of Britain in a European context of shifting cultural and religious boundaries.

Head of the Emperor Hadrian from the River Thames (2nd century AD).

left
Head of Christ from the Hinton St Mary mosaic, Roman Britain, 4th century AD, the earliest securely dated head of Christ.

right
Gold buckle from the Thetford Treasure (4th century AD).

Julius Caesar invades Britain (55 BC)	Constantine and Byzantium (306 AD)	Rome sacked (410 AD)

Roman Empire (27 BC–410 AD)

Pompeii buried (79 AD) Hadrian's Wall (120 AD)

BC/AD	100 AD	200 AD	300 AD	400 AD

Lycurgus Cup, Roman
glass, 4th century AD. (41)

The Franks Casket,
whalebone,
8th century AD. (41)

Early Medieval Europe,
Room 41

The continuing influence of
classical culture on Mediterranean Europe is shown by the
Lycurgus Cup and by the rich
civilisation of Byzantium *(cases
1–8; see also later icons in **42**).*
One strand in Northern
European culture is revealed by
the Anglo-Saxons in England and
the Sutton Hoo Ship Burial *(far
bay, cases 45–50),* an astonishing
20th-century discovery from a
royal grave field which included
Byzantine and other treasures.
An Anglo-Saxon king was buried
c.625 AD in a ship of which only
the impression and metal rivets
survived. As with the Welwyn

Garden City burial (**50**), this king
hoped for an afterlife of feasting
(cauldron and drinking horns,
silver tableware), and yet there
are also Christian spoons. This
was a time when Christianity
had not yet been securely re-
established in Britain, 200 years
after the demise of Rome. The
8th-century Franks Casket
(centre case) also combines
Christian and pagan subjects
with Runic inscriptions *(see also
case 39).* A Viking silver hoard
from Lancashire contained over
7,000 coins and other bullion
(case 33). Scandinavian Vikings
conquered and settled in many
parts of England, Scotland and
Ireland, and in northern France
(the Normans).

Helmet from the Sutton
Hoo Ship Burial, Anglo-
Saxon (7th century AD).
(**41**)

Sutton Hoo (c.625)

Charlemagne (c.760)

Anglo Saxons (c.500–1066)

Byzantium (306 –1453)

Lindisfarne Gospels (700)   Viking raids (c.750)   Book of Kells (800)

300 AD   600 AD   700 AD   800 AD   900 AD

Medieval Europe, *Room 42*
(may be affected by works from 2006/2007)

This introduces medieval art styles: Byzantine *(cases 1 and 2)* including icons and ivories; Romanesque and Gothic. The Byzantine empire, which was to extend right around the Mediterranean, begins with the Roman Emperor Constantine adopting Byzantium (renamed Constantinople, now Istanbul) as his capital in 330 AD. Ivories *(41, case 8)* give a glimpse of splendid buildings and decoration. Later, 14th-century icons *(42, cases 1–2)* range from a characterful St John the Baptist and St Peter, to the 'Triumph of orthodoxy' which depicts an icon claimed to have been painted by St Luke. Later icons from Crete and Russia are in *case 13.* A few decades later in 1453, Byzantium was captured by the Ottoman Turks *(see pp.36–7)* but its influence continued long afterwards.

The Lewis Chessmen *(case 3)*, probably Scandinavian from the mid-12th century, were found partly hidden beneath a sandbank on the Scottish island of Lewis in 1831, and show the continuing links of the northern world. In addition to much religious art in this gallery, secular objects display the splendour of royal courts: the Royal Gold Cup (c.1380, from France), aristocratic

One of the Lewis Chessmen (mid-12th century). **(42)**

The Royal Gold Cup, French (c.1380). **(42)**

left
Icon of St John the Baptist from Constantinople (c.1300). **(42)**

right
Ivory panel with archangel, Constantinople, 6th century AD. **(41, case 8)**

Norman conquest (1066) Tower of London	Gothic cathedrals (1100s–)		Portuguese explorers

Hundred Years' War with France (1337–1453)

Byzantium (306–1453)

| Crusades (1100s) | Westminster Abbey (c.1250) | Gutenberg and printing (1438) | Fall of Byzantium (1453) |

Ship clock, Prague
(c.1585). (44)

jewellery such as the Dunstable Swan Jewel (early 15th century) *(case 9)*, and paintings from the old royal palace of Westminster, converted for use as Parliament, and mostly burnt down in 1834.

Clocks and watches, **44**, cover the history of mechanical timekeeping and include an extraordinary ship clock made in Augsburg (c.1585) *(see Time tour, pp.72–3)*.

The Waddesdon Bequest, **45**, is a Rothschild collection: one of the most notable pieces is the reliquary made in Paris (c.1400) for the Duc de Berri to contain

what was thought to be one of the thorns from Christ's crown.

Renaissance, Baroque and Rococo art from Europe, **46**, includes Italian maiolica, Venetian enamelled glass, Huguenot silver *(case 14)*, jewellery *(cases 22–23)*, and pottery from Britain and Holland. The development of porcelain can be traced from its first successful production in Europe, in 1708 in Germany *(case 18)*. Superb examples of Chelsea porcelain, the 'Cleopatra' vases, are in *case 21*. In **47** are pieces from the Wedgwood factory *(cases 1–2)*, including a copy of the Portland Vase, and also the gold Portland Font.

left
The Holy Thorn Reliquary, France (c.1400–10). (45)

right
Detail from a 'Cleopatra' vase, Chelsea porcelain (1762). (46)

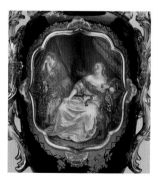

Renaissance Italy (c.1400)	Columbus (1492)	Reformation. Dürer	Drake, Raleigh, Frobisher	Shakespeare

Tudors in Britain (1485–1603)

Raphael and Michelangelo — Dutch Republic. Rembrandt, Delft (1600s)

1400 — 1500 — 1600

Jewellery from the Hull Grundy Gift is also shown here *(wallcases)* as well as in **46**. Western art of the 18th and 19th century was inspired not only by classical art *(e.g. case 4)* but also by cultures ranging from Islam to Japan. Room **48** shows the Museum actively collecting the 20th century with examples of modern design from Soviet Russia, the Bauhaus, America and Britain *(changing displays)*.

For more detail on these rooms see the Pottery tour *(pp.61–2)* and the Jewellery tour *(pp.53–4)*.

*Return to the Front hall via **47**, **41**, **36** and South stairs or lift from **35**.*

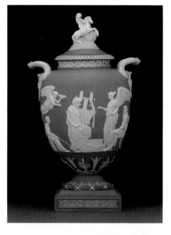

The 'Pegasus' Vase made and given by Wedgwood (1786). **(47)**

left
The gold Portland Font designed by Humphrey Repton (1797–8). **(47)**

bottom left
Gold waist buckle by Boucheron, Paris, 1900, from the Hull Grundy Gift. **(47)**

bottom right
Silver Bauhaus teapot designed by Marianne Brandt (c.1924). **(48)**

| Thirty Years' War (1618) | Louis XIV (1700) | | Industrial Revolution | French Revolution (1789) | | First World War (1914) |

Georgians (1714–1837) Victorians (1837–1901)

| Civil Wars (1640s) | Porcelain at Meissen (1709) | The British Museum (1753) Wedgwood | Napoleon (1815) | Russian Revolution (1917) |

1700   1800   1900

Tour 4
Asia and the Islamic world

From the Great Court go north through the
Wellcome Trust gallery (**24**) and then up the
stairs to the Hotung Gallery (**33**). To your left
is the display on South and South-East Asia,
mainly India; to your right is China.

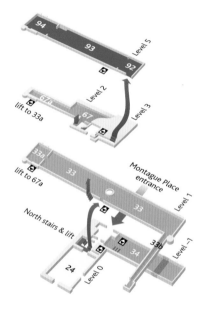

China, *Room 33 (right)*
*Begin with a chronological tour
of China.*

The Chinese invented mass-
production, notably in ceramics
(case 1), both for domestic
use and for making moulds for
bronzes. Bronzes (weapons, tools
and ritual objects) and jades
show how advanced early Chinese
technology was *(cases 1–12)*.
The earliest object here is a
jade of c.3500 BC *(case 2)*: jades
were thought to have magical,
protective qualities because
of their exceptional hardness
*(see also **33b**)*.
    A major civilisation was now
developing in the valley of the
Yellow River in north China: early
historical documents include
bronzes with inscriptions

Earliest pottery (Japan) (10,000 BC)	Early cultures (4000 BC)	Shang dynasty (1700 BC)	Buddha (c.563 BC)

Rice cultivation (6000 BC)	Yellow River Culture (2500 BC) Indus Valley (2500 BC)	Zhou period (1000 BC)	Confucius (451 BC)

7000 BC   2000 BC   1000 BC

recording battles and the award of titles *(case 6)*.

A strong, centralised state developed under the First Emperor (220 BC), who consolidated the Great Wall and was buried with his famous 'terracotta army'. China began to trade widely by sea and land: a remarkable Tang-period tomb group (8th century AD), in the centre *(case 47)*, includes the type of horses traded in exchange for Chinese silk along the Silk Route that extended west to Baghdad. *(Central Asia is featured in cases 65–67)* Fine silver also came east *(case 24)*.

Buddhism reached China from India in the earliest centuries AD and received state patronage, but its followers also suffered terrible persecution

(cases 19–22). At the end of the gallery are 15th-century wall paintings from a Buddhist temple and ceramic figures of a luohan (believed to have witnessed the Buddha's ascent to Nirvana) and guardians of heaven and hell.

China had a monopoly on porcelain production *(cases 27–29)* which was exported throughout Asia and to the West *(cases 39–42, 61–63)*. Lacquer *(case 43)* began as a protective coating for wooden boxes and leather armour, but turned into a decorative and highly elaborate art form. Jewellery for men and women *(case 52)* reflects the lavish court culture which survived *(cases 52–59)* until the revolutions of the 20th century destroyed it.

Porcelain flask, Ming dynasty (1426–35). (**33**)

Ceramic figure of an assistant to a judge of hell, Ming dynasty, 16th century. (**33**)

opposite page
Ritual bronze vessel in the form of a pair of rams, Shang dynasty (12th–11th century BC). (**33**)

left
Ceramic figure of a luohan (10th–12th century). (**33**)

Qin emperor, terracotta army, Great Wall (220 BC)

Chinese Revolutions

Tang (618–906)

Ming (1368–1644)

Qing (1644–1911)

Buddhism in China (65 AD)

BC/AD   1000   1300   1400   1500   1600   1700   1800   1900

Bronze figure of the
Hindu god Shiva
Nataraja, Chola period
(c.1100). (**33**)

South and South-East Asia, Room 33 (left)

South and South-East Asia is to your left as you enter from the North stairs.

The early urban culture of the Indus Valley (from c.2500 BC in modern Pakistan and north-west India) remains mysterious. You can see its script, still undeciphered, here on seals *(case 3)* that have been found as far away as ancient Iraq. From these roots developed what is now called Hinduism. The Hindu god Shiva is shown dancing *(case 37 in the centre)* in a remarkably expressive bronze, triumphing over ignorance in an arch of fire and time. Beyond, in stone which was originally brightly painted, he is with his consort Parvati. There are several images of the popular god Ganesh and the many forms of Vishnu *(cases 7–10)*.

Buddhism began in the 500s BC as a reaction to what Hinduism had become. Early Buddhist art particularly from Gandhara (modern Pakistan) *(cases 11–13)*, reflects the life of the Buddha. Also on display are sculptures from Buddhist shrines such as Sanchi *(case 14)* and Sarnath (in the centre), where the Buddha preached his first sermon, and especially from the 2nd and 3rd centuries AD at Amaravati, **33a** *(far end, behind glass screen)*.

left
Ganesh, Hindu god of good beginnings, and remover of obstructions. (**33**)

right
The Buddha teaching, from Sarnath (5th–6th century AD). (**33**)

Indus Valley (2500 BC)

Buddha (c.563 BC)

Alexander the Great (330s BC)

Cycladic Greece. Egypt. China (2500 BC)

2500 BC

1000 BC

A striking display on Nepal and Tibet *(cases 51–54)* includes exquisite Buddhist figures. Note also the 8th-century figure of the goddess Tara, from Sri Lanka, offering understanding and blessing *(in the centre of the gallery)*.

BUDDHISM

Buddhist reliquary from Bimaran, Afghanistan (1st–2nd century AD). **(33)**

In this gallery you can trace how, from its beginnings in India, Buddhism and Buddhist art took on a distinctive character in each country they reached. While the Chinese Amida Buddha on the North stairs is massive and authoritative, the Sri Lankan Tara is exquisitely expressive. Buddhism spread north west to Afghanistan *(see the reliquary left)*, and then along the Silk Road of Central Asia to China, and then Korea and Japan; to Nepal and Tibet and throughout South-East Asia. Buddhist art from the Dunhuang oasis on the Silk Road is one of the Museum's greatest treasures – brought back by Aurel Stein in the early 20th century. For conservation reasons these textiles and paintings cannot be on permanent display but some can be accessed on Museum websites. The earliest dated printed book (868 AD) is a Buddhist text from this site (now in the British Library).

Gilt bronze figure of Tara from Sri Lanka (8th century AD). **(33)**

right
One of the drum slabs from and showing the great stupa at Amaravati (2nd–3rd century AD). **(33a)**

left
Gilded lacquer figure of the Buddha from Burma (late 18th/early 19th century) with 20th-century lacquered and gilded base. **(33)**

Muhammad (622 AD) Angkor Wat, Cambodia (1120) Taj Mahal (1632)

Amaravati (100 BC–300 AD)

Buddhism in China (65 AD) Chola dynasty bronzes (1000 AD) Mughals (1526)

JAPAN

Woodblock print of Kabuki actors by Sharaku (1794).

Ivory netsuke of a tiger (19th century) – a toggle to secure objects hung from the sash round the waist, in the absence of pockets.

Japan, *Rooms 92–94*

*Leave **33** and take the North stairs or lift to level 5.*

Highlights of the Japanese collection are displayed in **92–94**. The collection is remarkably comprehensive, ranging from early archaeology and Buddhist art to prints, paintings and decorative arts such as ceramics and lacquer. There are coloured woodblock prints by artists such as Hokusai and Sharaku, famous for depicting Kabuki actors, and netsuke – ivory toggles for fastening objects from the sash of a kimono. Swords and armour as well as netsuke, contemporary graphics and ceramics can often be seen. The Way of Tea is sometimes presented in the Tea House here.

*Return to the North stairs and go to level 2, or lift to level 1 (wheelchair access from **33**) or to level 3, and then stairs to the Korea Foundation Gallery. (**67**)*

Jomon period (10,000 BC)		Heian period			Meiji period
				Edo (Tokyo) period (1680–1868)	
	Buddhism (500s AD)		Europeans in Japan (1500s)		
10,000 BC	BC/AD	1300	1500	1700	1900

Korea, *Room 67*

*From **33** (wheelchair access) take the North stairs to level 2, or lift to level 3 and then stairs.*

Korea has a unique and fascinating culture which incorporates native ideas and techniques and influences from other parts of Asia, especially Buddhist art from China. Highlights include 5th- to 6th-century royal gold earrings *(case 4)* from the capital of Silla in south-east Korea; a late 12th-century celadon water sprinkler *(case 6)*, used for purifying the ground during Buddhist ceremonies; and a 13th-century lacquer inlaid sutra box *(case 7)* – one of only eight remaining, made to contain sacred Buddhist scriptures. The 17th-century 'Full-Moon' jar *(case 14)* is admired for its natural simplicity and purity. The Sarangbang (constructed in the Museum by Korean craftsmen) would have been used by the gentlemen of the house as a study and for receiving visitors.

Changing displays (**67a**) feature contemporary art collected from both North and South Korea.

Korean white porcelain 'Full-Moon' jar, Choson dynasty (1392–1910). (**67**)

opposite page, left
Detail from a lacquer writing-box with gold, shell, silver and mother-of-pearl decoration, 17th century.

opposite page, right
Samurai armour (17th–19th century) incorporating thick steel plate to withstand bullets from guns introduced by the Portuguese.

left
Guardian king, guarding the entrance to a Buddhist temple, Choson dynasty, dated 1796–1820. (**67**)

Bronze Age (c.1000 BC)

3 Kingdoms (c.57 BC–668 AD)   Koryo dynasty (918–1392)   Choson dynasty (1392–1910)

Unified Silla period (668–935)

| 1000 BC | BC/AD | 1000 | 1300 | 1600 | 1900 |

Enamelled glass mosque lamp from Egypt or Syria, 14th century. (**34**)

Islamic art, *Room 34*

Return via the North stairs or lift to the Addis Gallery of Islamic Art, by the Montague Place Entrance.

This gallery displays aspects of the art of Islam, from the 7th century AD to the present day, and from Spain to India. The arrangement is mainly chronological, with western Islam – Egypt, Syria, Iraq and Turkey – on the left as you go down the stairs, and eastern Islam – Iran, Afghanistan and India – to the right.

The prophet Muhammad was born at Mecca in c.570 AD. Islamic history begins with his flight to Medina in 622 AD. Texts from the Koran appear on many objects here such as the Iranian bowl in *case 6*, and the tiles in *case 2*. The Dome of the Rock in Jerusalem is holy for Muslims: an enamelled glass mosque lamp from this shrine is in *case 21 (on the left)*, as well as rock crystals, highly valued in medieval Europe.

Three major Islamic empires are represented here, including Ottoman Turkey. Having captured the capital of the Christian Byzantine empire (modern Istanbul, ancient Contantinople) in 1453, the Ottoman Turks posed a major threat to Christian Europe for the next 250 years, reaching as far as the walls of Vienna and encircling the Mediterranean from Greece to North Africa. Ottoman pottery from Iznik

Ceramic basin made at Iznik, Ottoman Turkey (c.1550). (**34**)

Damascus, Baghdad

Muhammad's flight from Mecca (622)

Fatimid period, Cairo

500 AD   600 AD   700 AD   800 AD   900 AD   1000

(displayed in cases 27–35) transformed Chinese motifs and developed new designs and colours.

Art from Iran in the Safavid era (1502–1736) is shown on the right-hand side of the gallery, including tiles from Isfahan in case 25. An 18th-century Iranian astrolabe – a navigational aide – which belonged to the Museum's founder, Hans Sloane, is now displayed in the Enlightenment Gallery (1).

The third of these major empires – the Mughals – established themselves in India from the 1520s until they were finally removed by the British in the 19th century. Their most notable monument is the Taj Mahal, to whose builder, Shah Jahan, one of the jades in case 41 is dedicated. In case 43 is a delightful jade terrapin probably commissioned by his father, the Emperor Jahangir.

The impact of Islam on European culture has been considerable: in science, maths and navigation, and in technologies such as ceramics. In case 47 there is lustreware from Spain when under Moorish rule and after the Reconquest in the late 15th century (see Pottery tour, pp.59, 61).

The Museum's textile collection includes Palestinian and Central Asian material; the Africa Galleries (25) include Egyptian and Tunisian textiles, and Moroccan pots.

left
Jade terrapin from Mughal India (early 17th century). (34)

right
Astrolabe from Iran (1712). (1)

Mamluk, Egypt	Ottomans take Byzantium (1453)		Mughal India (1526–1858)
			Safavid Iran (1502–1736)
Crusades (1100s)	Alhambra, Granada. Moorish Spain (1350s)	Reformation. Charles V (1500s)	Last Turkish siege of Vienna (1683)
1100	1200	1300	1400	1500	1600	1700

Tour 5
Africa and the Americas

To find out about early Africa and the civilisations of ancient Egypt and Nubia take tour 2 (pp.16–21).

This tour starts from the Great Court: go through the North door and take the stairs down in the Wellcome Trust Gallery (**24**), or West or East lifts from the Great Court (adjacent to the bookshop).

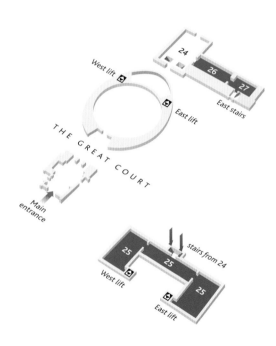

Africa, *Room 25*

The Sainsbury African galleries are arranged thematically, beginning with a changing display of contemporary art. The living tradition of masquerades is illustrated by 19th- and 20th-century masks and the steel sculptures of Sokari Douglas Camp, a Nigerian artist based in London. The Museum collects actively in many parts of the world, and you can see more examples upstairs in **24**.

SEE ALSO

- Prehistoric Africa in **36** (case 1)
- Material from Roman Africa (**70**), including crocodile armour (case 18) and mosaics from Carthage (cases 29, 33)
- European links with Africa in **42** (case 11) and **46** (case 15)
- Living and dying in **24** (pp.80–1)

| Predynastic Egypt (5500 BC) | Old Kingdom Egypt (2686 BC) | Kush, Sudan (2500 BC) | Saharan trade (1000 BC) | Meroë, Sudan (700 BC) | Carthage, Tunisia (500 BC) | Nok, Nigeria. Iron smelting (400 BC) | Greek and Roman Egypt (332 BC) |

| 5000 BC | 2000 BC | BC/AD |

Turn right and then left to see brass plaques and ivories from the West African kingdom of Benin, Nigeria *(case 4)*. This was one of the first African cultures to be experienced by Europeans, following the arrival of the Portuguese in the 1400s. The 16th- to 17th-century brass plaques decorated the king's palace; the ivory salt cellar *(case 5)* was made for sale to the Portuguese who are depicted here and in the hair of the ivory pectoral mask.

The 16th-century queen mother head, also from Benin, is a particularly expressive piece of brass sculpture. It depicts Queen Idia, and is one of the most famous images in African art. She is remembered even today as a leader in war as well as for her healing skills. Also in Nigeria, the Yoruba kingdom developed from the 10th century: the brass head of a king comes from Ife and is of an earlier date than the Benin pieces *(case 4)*. Also from West Africa come vibrant textiles such as the Kente cloth made by the Asante people of Ghana.

Ivory salt-cellar from Benin, depicting bearded Portuguese and one of the ships in which they arrived in West Africa – some of the earliest 'tourist' art. (16th century). **(25)**

opposite page
Ivory pectoral mask from Benin, Nigeria, with Portuguese heads in the hair (late 15th–early 16th century). **(25)**

left
Bronze head of a queen mother from Benin (16th century). **(25)**

right
Brass head from Ife, Nigeria (12th–15th century). **(25)**

Christian Ethiopia and Egypt (400 AD)   Portuguese in Africa (1498)   Dutch settle at the Cape (1600)   Asante empire (Ghana) (1700)
Benin bronzes and ivories (1500)

Ife (Nigeria), Ghana (800 AD)   Mali (1100 AD)   First African slaves in America (1518)   'Scramble for Africa' by Europeans (1880s)
Arab invasions. Islamic Egypt (969 AD)   Ottoman Turks replace Mamluks (1517)

1000   1100   1500   1600   1900

The lyre *(case 11)* is from Sudan – its shape that of ancient Egyptian lyres in tomb paintings. It is a type still played at weddings and by shepherds. This one has been customised with cowries, coins, glass and metal. *Now retrace your steps to the centre of the galleries and go on to the far side and the wood carving section.* Some figures represent ancestors, such as the 17th-century founder of the Congo kingdom of Kuba in Central Africa *(case 12)*. The Nkisi figure of a fierce double-headed animal (c.1900) *(case 14)* has packs of medicinal materials attached to it; and nails have been driven in to seek help in pursuing wrongdoers.

The arrival in Europe of art from the Congo began to show that African culture had developed without European stimulus.

The pots in the adjacent gallery come from many traditions: they combine utility with beauty and may symbolically contain the spirits of ancestors, gods or even diseases *(see Pottery tour p.63).*

The age of colonisation is reflected in many exhibits: the quilted horse-armour was captured from the Sudanese in battle in 1898; a wooden carving shows a British colonial officer arriving at the Yoruba king's palace to collect taxes *(on the wall opposite case 12).*

Earlier colonisations and the changing relations of Africa to the rest of the world can be explored in many parts of the

below left
Lyre from the Sudan (19th century). **(25)**

below right
Nkisi figure from the Democratic Republic of Congo (c.1900). **(25)**

Old Kingdom Egypt (2686 BC)   Saharan trade (1000 BC)

Carthage, Tunisia (500 BC)   Greek and Roman Egypt (332 BC)

Predynastic Egypt (5500 BC)   Kush, Sudan (2500 BC)   Meroë, Sudan (700 BC)   Nok, Nigeria. Iron smelting (400 BC)

Museum *(see the box on p.38)*. Among the exquisite ivories from Nimrud (9th–8th century BC) **(57)** *(see p.45)* is an image of an African being devoured by a lion, a Phoenician piece probably originally from North Africa. One of the greatest of the ancient Greek colonies was in Libya at Cyrene, a fertile oasis between coast and desert. A statue of Apollo from the sanctuary there is in **22**, as is the remarkable Berber head in bronze illustrated here. It was originally extraordinarily lifelike: lips overlaid with copper sheet, teeth of white bone, separately cast eyelashes and glass eyes with enamelled whites.

These represent idealised images of Africa. By contrast the bronze head of the Roman

Emperor Augustus in **70** *(Upper floor)*, c.27–25 BC *(see p.15)*, is the result of a violent African backlash to imperial rule. It probably comes from an over-life-sized statue of the emperor who defeated Cleopatra and Antony and took control of Egypt. Raiding tribesmen from Meroë, Sudan *(see pp.20–21)*, decapitated the statue. They deliberately buried the head under the steps of a temple commemorating their successful raids. Meanwhile Roman portrait art was superimposed on traditional Egyptian mummies, just as Roman culture and power were imposed on Egypt – see the mummy of Artemidorus (2nd century AD) in **62** *(p.14)*.

From medieval Africa comes a mystery object in **42** *(case 11)*

Wooden figure of the 17th-century founder of the Kuba dynasty with a mancala game-board (c.18th century) from the Democratic Republic of Congo. **(25)**

left
Bronze head of a Berber from North Africa, Greek, Cyrene, c.350–300 BC. **(22)**

right
Ugandan pots (19th–20th century) made for the Baganda king's palace. **(25)**

Christian Ethiopia and Egypt (400 AD)

Portuguese in Africa (1498)
Benin bronzes and ivories (1500)

Dutch settle at the Cape (1600)   Asante empire, Ghana (1700)

Ife (Nigeria), Ghana (800 AD)   Mali (1100 AD)   First African slaves in America (1518)   'Scramble for Africa' by Europeans (1880s)
Arab invasions. Islamic Egypt (969 AD)   Ottoman Turks replace Mamluks (1517)

1000   1100   1500   1600   1900

NORTH AMERICA

Native North American mask from the Northwest Coast. (**26**)

– a 14th-century English brass jug traded across the Sahara to Ghana and used as an exotic object by the Ashante kings from whom it was taken in the 19th century. Like so many objects in the Museum it shows how the world has always been more interconnected than we often realise.

North America, *Room 26*

Now return to the Main floor above to the Wellcome Trust Gallery (24) and find the door to 26: J.P. Morgan Chase Gallery of North America.

'First Peoples, First Contacts' celebrates the diversity of Native American culture with a changing display from the Museum's rich and historic collections – dating from 10,000 years ago to the present day. Turn to your right and start with some of the material here from the Northwest Coast brought back from Captain Cook's voyage in 1778, especially masks. This tradition of mask-making continues today.

Robes of goat wool and cedar bark were worn by high-ranking chiefs at feasts and are decorated with the animal crests of their owners *(see also 24)*. Move along to your right to the Southeast and Northeast Woodlands, lands of the Iroquois, Creek and Cherokee. A modern 'Mohawk Lunch Pail' combines images of Native and urban America *(case 2)*. Other Native peoples reflected here include the Navajo and Apache of the

'Mohawk Lunch Pail' by Ric Glazer Danay (1983) combines contemporary American images with Native references. (**26**)

First evidence of humans	Agriculture (700 AD)	Norse settlements	First African slaves (1518) Columbus (1492)	First colonies (1600s)	Lewis and Clark cross North America (1804)
c.10,000–6000 BC	200 BC–600 AD	1000–1300 AD			
	Hopewell period Burial mounds (Ohio)	Mississippian period (1000)	Frobisher in the Arctic (1570s) Captain Cook on the Northwest Coast	Independence (1776)	Civil War (1861–5)
10,000 BC	BC/AD	1000			1800

Southwest (where the Museum collects contemporary jewellery and ceramics) and the Blackfoot of the plains. The Arctic and Subarctic collections are particularly rich, dating back to early European contact with the Cree, Dene and Inuit. A Haida totem pole is by the East stairs, *(through 27)*. Other material is in **24**.

Mexico, *Room 27*

Highlights include Aztec turquoise mosaics (15th to 16th century AD), notably a double-headed serpent and a human skull decorated in mosaic and with realistic eyes and teeth. On the back wall are sculpted lintels from much earlier Maya temples at Yaxchilan (8th century AD),

such as Lintel 16 in which Bird Jaguar (a Maya ruler) stands over a kneeling captive noble who has been stripped of his finery. In the centre of the gallery striking Huaxtec figures (10th–15th century AD) come from the Gulf Coast. The Olmec culture (1200–400 BC) is one of the first great art styles in the Americas. Its monumentality is glimpsed even in much smaller pieces like the jade axe combining the features of jaguar and caiman.

Collections from modern Mexico and Andean South America are included in the Wellcome Trust Gallery (**24**).

above
Limestone Maya Lintel 16 from Yaxchilan ('Place of the Split Sky'), Mexico, c.755–70 AD. (**27**)

left
Double-headed serpent (15th–16th century), Mixtec-Aztec, from Mexico. Rare turquoise was reserved for ritual objects like this to be worn by priests and rulers, symbolising fertility. (**27**)

Olmecs (c.1200 BC)	Pyramids at Teotihuacan (150–200 AD)					
		Maya (c.200 BC–1000 AD)		Incas (1200–1534)	Aztecs (1370–1519)	
Earliest metalwork in South America (c.1500 BC)	Calendar (260-day) (700 BC) Nasca (c.200 BC)	Huaxtecs (900 AD)		Conquests by Pizarro (1519) and Cortes (1534)		
1500 BC	1000 BC	BC/AD	1000	1300	1400	1500

Animals

Greek lion in the Great Court, from Knidos. Once part of a monumental tomb above the sea at a cliff edge – its eyes were probably inset with glass to catch the light. (**Great Court**)

The spirits of the animal kingdom roam the Museum. Ancient cultures show affection and fear in their depiction of animals, giving some divine status, particularly in ancient Egypt and India.

Main floor

A Greek lion from Knidos (late 4th–early 3rd century BC) presides over the Great Court. From Ancient Iraq are lifelike lions from Nimrud (**6**, **57**, *Upper floor*) and lions are hunted in the Assyrian friezes (**10**). An Egyptian lion from Sudan is in the Egyptian sculpture gallery (**4**). A bull from the legend of the Minotaur in Minoan Crete is in **12**, along with bold sea creatures on pots.

left
Human-headed, winged bull and genie from Khorsabad, Assyria (c.710 BC). (**10**)

right
An Assyrian lion is released from its cage (mid-7th century BC). (**10**)

A mix of real and imagined animals such as gryphons appear in Greek art of all kinds *(from 13)* including coins. Proud Greek horses process up to the Acropolis in 5th-century Athens *(18)* and pull the chariot of the moon goddess across the night sky on the pediment of the Parthenon. Mythical creatures – part bird, fish, bull and man – stand guard over ancient Assyrian palaces *(10/23 and 7/8)*.

The Egyptians venerated many animals, notably the baboon *(centre of 4)*, the scarab beetle *(north end of 4)* and the cat *(61, Upper floor)*. Mummified animals are in **62**.

In Asia ceramic camels and horses trek along the Silk Road **(33)**, while mythical dragons, symbols of the emperor and of spring, decorate pots and enamelled jars. Jade animals **(33, 33b)** were sewn into ancient Chinese shrouds and later became a purely decorative art. In India serpents and elephants venerate the Buddha at Amaravati **(33a)**. The Hindu god Ganesh is elephant-headed, the bull Nandi venerates Shiva, and Vishnu is variously a boar and a giant fish **(33)**. From Mughal India **(34)** come especially expressive animals carved from precious stones *(case 41)*, such as the jade terrapin. Animals on zodiac and other Islamic coins are in *case 44*.

One of the ivories from Nimrud (Iraq), 8th century BC. **(57)**

left
Jade terrapin from Mughal India (early 17th century). **(34)**

right
Enamelled dragon jar, Chinese, Ming dynasty (1426–35). Five claws denote that these are imperial dragons – the jar was intended for use in a palace. **(33)**

Ivory netsuke of a tiger (19th century) – a toggle to secure objects hung from the sash round the waist, in the absence of pockets. (**92–94**)

In Africa (**25**) there are cheetahs from Benin, elephant masks from Cameroon, and a double-headed creature from the Congo – a nkisi figure – into which you hammer nails to ask for help in tracking down enemies and wrongdoers. Ashante gold weights made of brass are from 18th- to 19th-century Ghana.

Native North Americans (**26**) include many animal, fish and bird symbols on masks, soapstone carvings, jewellery and totem poles *(by the East stairs, beyond **27**)*. The thunder of the vanished buffalo herds of the North American plains hangs in the air. In Mesoamerica (**27**) it is the squeal of hairless dogs,

bred by the Maya like we breed chickens, to eat. In west Mexico dogs, like the pottery one on show, were believed to accompany the dead into the underworld. Serpents figure prominently in Aztec art, double-headed in mosaic, and with terrifying realism as a coiled stone rattlesnake. Also Aztec is an onyx spider monkey with red eyes.

Upper floor

Animals figure in European art from cave paintings to the age of Picasso, particularly in the metalwork of northern Europe, such as chariot fittings and objects for feasting and drinking.

left
Nkisi figure from the Democratic Republic of Congo (c.1900). (**25**)

opposite page
Bronze flesh fork with swans and ravens, from Dunaverny, Co. Antrim, Ireland, c.800 BC. (**50**)

The boar was an important warrior symbol in both Celtic Europe and Anglo-Saxon England (**41**), where it appears in the Sutton Hoo Ship Burial. The Celts believed that boars had supernatural powers and could also bring death and disaster.

In **42**, on the rare wooden gittern (a plucked musical instrument), you can see medieval pigs being fed acorns (c.1285 AD). Animals figure in heraldry from medieval England – the Dunstable Swan Jewel (c.1400) is also in **42**. Renaissance medals (**46**), like Greek coins, often feature animal emblems.

Bronze horse mask from Stanwick, Yorkshire (c.50–100 AD), probably part of a Celtic chariot ornament. (**50**)

below
Double-headed serpent (15th–16th century), Mixtec-Aztec, from Mexico. Rare turquoise was reserved for ritual objects like this to be worn by priests and rulers, symbolising fertility. (**27**)

Jewellery

*Begin on the Upper floor (stairs or lift from the Great Court and then across the bridge) in **56**, Early Mesopotamia.*

This tour will take you from the ancient Near East and Egypt to Greece and Rome (on the Upper floor), and then down to the Main floor, resuming with Europe on the Upper floor (p.52), Asia, the Americas and Africa (p.55). You may wish to choose among these options or break up the tour with coffee or lunch.

Ancient World, *Upper floor*

In room **56** *cases 6, 10, 12, 13–14* have Sumerian court jewellery from the death-pits of Ur (Iraq) from c.2500 BC. It would be difficult to wear more jewellery than that in *case 10*, and the lady involved was not a queen but an attendant, buried with her mistress. The materials are gold and red carnelian (from India) and blue lapis lazuli (from Afghanistan). Important Sumerian men often wore jewellery too, as did ancient Egyptian, Assyrian and Indian men. The jewellery of Ur influenced that of early Greece, both in the choice of exotic imported materials, and in technology. Granulation was introduced at Ur – a technique

Gold armlet from the Oxus Treasure, with horned and bird-headed creatures. Originally inlaid with precious stones (5th–4th century BC) from Iran. (**52**)

of soldering minute grains to a background, usually all in gold.

From ancient Iran comes the stunning Oxus Treasure, which dates from the 5th–4th century BC. The gold armlets are in the form of winged griffins, and the empty cells or cloisons were originally inlaid with coloured material. You can also see this technique used in the Sutton Hoo Ship Burial (**41**) and in Chinese enamels (**33**).

Jewellery is also shown in detail on busts from Palmyra, an oasis city in Syria, where Rome and Iran met through trade. From **56** go into **63** and then left into **62** to see ancient Egyptian jewellery. Jewellery was worn by the dead, and their coffins and mummy portraits also show them wearing it when alive (*e.g. a Roman lady in* **62**, *case 17, by the door*). In **62** are amulets for the dead (*back of case 23*) and a collar of faience (crushed quartz glazed in various colours, usually to imitate semi-precious stones, sometimes called 'glazed composition'). In **61** *case 36* displays collars of gold, glass, coloured stones and faience. A miniature enamel wig shows how diadems were worn.

In the upper Greek and Roman galleries you can trace distinctive jewellery styles around the Mediterranean including those of the Etruscans, pre-Roman inhabitants of Italy (**71**).

Lady from Palmyra, Syria, late 2nd century AD. Her lavish jewellery reflects the wealth of a city grown rich from the caravan trade across the Syrian desert.

Cases 17, 22, 27, 29 display jewellery. On her sarcophagus, Seianti Hanunia Tlesnasa is shown wearing gold jewellery – tiara, earrings, necklace, bracelets and rings *(case 15)*.

The Roman empire (**70**) extended in all directions, and there is jewellery here from provinces such as Judaea *(case 26)* and a remarkably well-preserved Egyptian garland of flowers *(case 29)*, of the kind imitated in ancient Egyptian jewellery. Cameos, like that of Augustus, were avidly collected in Renaissance and later Europe, and inspired jewellers *(see **47**)*. Room **69** (Greek and Roman Life) has a display on jewellery *(cases 28–29)*.

Return to the South stairs and either continue to Europe (p.52), from prehistory to modern, or return to the Main floor below.

Ancient World, *Main floor*

On the Main floor start in **12** *(case 6)* with Minoan-style jewellery probably from the Greek island of Aigina (1750–1500 BC). Earrings and necklaces feature snakes, monkeys, greyhounds and owls, and a male figure known as 'the master of animals'. The materials include amethyst, carnelian, jasper and lapis lazuli. Opposite *(in case 8)* is a later gold and carnelian necklace from Cyprus showing Eastern as well

Etruscan terracotta sarcophagus (c.250–200 BC) from a period when the Etruscans had been assimilated into the Roman world. (**71**)

as Mycenaean Greek influences. In the next room (**13**) are rings, necklaces, brooches and gold foil diadems from 1100 to 700 BC; and gems like flattened almonds. A treasure from Rhodes includes the ancient Near Eastern 'mistress of animals' transformed into the Greek goddess Artemis.

At the end of this sequence of galleries, Hellenistic jewellery (**22**) incorporates new ideas like the reef knot, earring styles from Iran and inlays of coloured stone and glass. In *case 5* are exquisitely fine necklaces and earrings, and a gold oak wreath (350–300 BC), of a type worn in religious processions or by winners of musical contests.

Returning briefly to the ancient Near East, you can see Assyrian kings on reliefs in adjacent galleries *(e.g. between* **4** *and* **23***)* wearing earrings, necklaces, bracelets and animal-headed armlets, the forerunners of the lavish one in the Oxus Treasure (**52**) that you saw earlier. See also the Stela of Ashurnasirpal in the Great Court *(by the West café)*.

*To continue with the tour take the South stairs or lift to the Upper floor (**36**).*

left
Cameo of Augustus (27 BC–14 AD), sardonyx with a jewelled diadem added in the Middle Ages. (**70**)

right
Minoan gold pendant from the Aigina Treasure (c.1750–1500 BC). (**12**)

Europe – prehistory to modern

At the top of the South stairs, start in **36** with gold jewellery and adornment from all over Europe such as the neck-ring from Sintra, Portugal (*case 3*). The design of this Bronze Age collar shows influences from as far away as Scandinavia – it was possibly for a child or woman. Prehistoric jewellery also used bone, shell, pebbles and semi-precious stones.

In Celtic Europe (*temporary display in* **2**), you can see the continuing tradition of highly conspicuous jewellery for men as for women. Torcs are a characteristic Celtic sign of status and wealth, worn round the neck. Made in complex clay moulds, torcs are found in Spain and Portugal as well as Britain. Brooches to fasten cloaks on one or both sides are found across the Celtic world from Ireland to Hungary and Turkey.

In Roman Britain (*temporary display in* **2**), buried treasures give us a glimpse of the lavish jewellery made in Britain during this period, or brought from elsewhere in Europe. The late Roman Thetford Treasure includes a very rare gold belt buckle showing a dancing satyr holding grapes; the rings incorporate woodpeckers and dolphins in their design. Roman style, taste and production in jewellery were maintained particularly at Constantinople (modern Istanbul), at the centre of

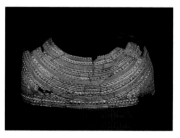

left
Gold cape from Mold, Wales, made from a single sheet of gold, c.1900–1600 BC. (**2**)

right
Celtic torc from Snettisham, Norfolk (1st century BC) – eight strands of gold (each of eight wires) twisted together. (**50**)

the Byzantine empire. In **41** Byzantine and other late Antique jewellery includes a gold body chain (c.600 AD) from Egypt.

The Sutton Hoo Ship Burial (**41**) shows Anglo-Saxon England in contact with Byzantium. The red garnets in this king's shoulder clasps came from India or Afghanistan and are interspersed with blue glass in gold filigree cloisons – all evidence of both aesthetic and technical sophistication. Other finds of jewellery come from cemeteries, especially in Kent.

The Fuller Brooch *(case 36)* is a large silver disc brooch probably from the time of Alfred the Great, and is decorated with illustrations of the five senses in niello (a black compound of various metals). A huge Viking-period 'thistle' brooch (from Penrith in Cumbria) is 50cm in length *(case 33)*. This is portable wealth at its most spectacular.

In the Medieval Gallery (**42**) *(case 9)* is the Noah cameo which belonged to the Medici. The early 15th-century Dunstable Swan Jewel is gold covered with enamel, and was pinned to the hat or dress as a sign of support for the House of Lancaster during the Wars of the Roses. Other notable pieces of European jewellery are in the Waddesdon Bequest (**45**), including the Lyte Jewel awarded by James I to the man who demonstrated his descent from the Trojans (1610) *(case 4)*.

In **46** Tudor and Stuart jewels

left
Gold buckle from the late Roman Thetford Treasure, Norfolk (4th century AD). It was possibly part of the stock of a jeweller or merchant buried for safekeeping.

right
Shoulder-clasps of gold, garnet and glass from the Anglo-Saxon Sutton Hoo Ship Burial (c.625–30 AD). (**41**)

include the Phoenix Jewel of Elizabeth I (c.1570–80) framed with Tudor roses *(case 6 on the right)*. Part of the jeweller's hoard from Cheapside, London (c.1600–40) is in *case 11 (halfway along the gallery)*, including amethysts carved as bunches of grapes. Also in *case 11* is the insignia of the Order of the Garter, the greatest honour from the British sovereign – an example is worn by Prince Rupert, nephew of Charles I, on the stoneware bust nearby.

In the 17th century taste in dress changed and jewellery became far less elaborate. The taste of the 18th century is reflected in the remarkable Hull Grundy Gift. In **46**, *cases 22–23* are of gem-set and gold jewels, and enamels. Room **47** shows neo-classical jewellery *(cases 3–4)*, inspired by archaeology *(case 11)*, nature *(case 8)* and Japan *(case 12)*. It includes jewels by great 19th-century makers such as Castellani and Tiffany.

Jewellery of the 20th century is often displayed in **48**.

left
Prince Rupert wearing the Order of the Garter – stoneware bust by John Dwight (1670s). **(46)**

right
Gold waist buckle by Boucheron, Paris, 1900, from the Hull Grundy Gift. **(47)**

Asia, the Americas and Africa

Leave the Great Court through the North door and the Wellcome Trust Gallery (24), and go up the stairs to 33 (Hotung Gallery).

The use of jade goes right back to before 3500 BC in China *(see case 2)*. It was thought to be magical and was used especially to protect the dead, sewn as amulets into the shroud *(see window case 8)*. Cross the gallery to the right to see Chinese court jewellery from the later Ming and Qing dynasties *(case 52)*: gold nail-guards for the exceptionally long nails of court ladies, and hair pins and ornaments. There are ornaments too for men *(on the other side)* – jade belt ornaments and dragon plaques for senior court officials – and a delicate crown. Chinese jade has its own display in **33b** *(turn right at the far end of the Chinese section)*.

The art of the Indian jeweller can be seen in **33** *(cases 4 and 18)* and in **34** *(floor below)*, *case 42*, at the far end of the room. Korean jewellery is shown in **67** *(access from the North stairs)*.

Mexican ceremonial regalia, including Olmec and Mayan jades and Mixtec gold, is in **27**. North American jewellery in **26** includes recently collected work from the Southwest. Asante gold pieces from Ghana are among the most striking African jewellery in **25** *(Lower floor)*.

left
Ivory netsuke of a tiger – a toggle to secure objects hung from a sash round the waist, in the absence of pockets. Japan, 19th century. (**92-4**)

right
Turquoise serpent. Mixtec-Aztec, from Mexico, 15th–16th century. (**27**)

Money

The HSBC Money Gallery (**68**) is an unusually wide-ranging introduction to its subject – its exhibits include money boxes and children's teeth (for the tooth fairy) as well as Chinese pots, credit cards, prehistoric gold and, of course, coins.

SEE ALSO

Coins are also displayed in other galleries:
- Greece (**13**, **24**, **71–73**)
- Rome (**70**)
- Ancient Near East (**55**)
- Asia (**33**)
- Islam (**34**, **65**)
- Europe (**41–42**, **46–48**)

Start in *case 1*, nearest to **37** and the South stairs. The earliest urban civilisations have the earliest monetary systems, not surprisingly. For example, Mesopotamia (ancient Near East) used specified amounts of metals or grain from c.3000 BC *(section 1 in case 1)*. The Chinese were using cowrie shells *(section 1 in case 1)* as money from c.1500 (later uses are shown in *case 19*).

The first coins are from Lydia (modern Turkey), made of gold and silver alloy, and from China *(section 4 in case 1)*. These are of bronze in the shape of tools, c.600 BC, and were strung together through a centre hole.

Money can take many forms. In *case 3* you can see how silver and other materials were used

An example of one of the many coin hoards discovered in Britain that shed light on the country's early history.

before coinage in Egypt and the ancient Near East, and in *cases 8 and 9* how copper rings, cloth and shells were used instead of coins in Africa and the Americas.

In *case 7* (nos 11,12) is a silver Roman coin (c.45 BC) of the goddess Juno Moneta, who gave her name to 'money'. Tools for making coins are shown on the back. Early Indian coins are important evidence for the spread of Buddhism. Early Islamic coins follow quickly from the age of Muhammad himself, c.630 AD *(cases 8 and 12)*, with the inscription 'There is no god but God'.

As well as inventing paper, the Chinese invented paper money (10th century AD) *(case 8)*.

The first paper money in the West, in Sweden, followed 700 years later *(see case 19 for later examples)*. Technology is explained from *cases 14–15* onwards. Plastic money begins with the first credit cards in the USA in 1946 and for many of us today the 'hole in the wall' is our main supply of money *(case 17)*. *Case 18* shows money boxes and other contemporary items.

Temporary displays in this gallery include new archaeology: coin hoards are often discovered when ploughing, on building sites and by the use of metal detectors, or even in shipwrecks. Room **69a** has changing exhibitions on a great variety of subjects relating to money and medals.

Children learn about money at a family event.

Pottery

There are pots and ceramic figures in most areas of the Museum. Here is a selection designed to show continuities and connections across cultures: Asian, Classical, European and African. To see the evolution of one of the world's major ceramic traditions, start with China in **33**, Hotung Gallery (north from the Great Court via **24**).

Figure of a luohan, Liao dynasty (10th–12th century), an image of serene enlightenment, one of an original set of eight. (**33**)

Asia

The earliest known fired clay objects come from Japan (c.10,000 BC). Later the Chinese invented quality mass-production pottery, also using clay moulds. In *case 1*, on your right, is a 15th-century porcelain flask in blue and white. No one else in the world could produce anything like that at the time, nor for another three centuries in Europe. Compare it with a prehistoric pot (*case 2*) and you can see the evolution of Chinese pottery over 1600 years – a culture with the right kinds of clay and the technological grasp to exploit them. Early porcelain is in *cases 27 and 28* with the very rare Ru ware imitating jade in *case 29*. Especially fine later porcelain is

left
Porcelain flask, Ming dynasty (1426–35). (**33**)

right
Porcelain vase with flowering peach branch, Qing dynasty (18th century). (**33**)

in *case 57* on the other side of the gallery. In the centre *(case 47)* are figures from a Tang tomb – camels, horses and guardians. At the far end is the stoneware figure of a ferocious assistant to a judge of hell, with aubergine, green and olive glazes *(see p.31)*, and the large lead-glazed earthenware figure of a Buddhist luohan.

China exported porcelain and other ceramics throughout Asia and Europe until the 18th century, when European porcelain developed first in Meissen. *Cases 61 and 63* show Chinese and European ceramics side by side *(also in the European Gallery, 46)*.

China's influence on the pottery of the Islamic world is clear in **34**, where the Iznik potters of Ottoman Turkey began by copying Chinese blue and white in the 15th century and then developed their own styles and colours *(cases 27–35)*. Nearby in *case 47* you can see the impact of North African Moorish potters in Spain, which in turn influenced Renaissance Italian maiolica *(see **46**)*. Ceramic tiles as seen in this gallery are a feature of many Islamic mosques and palaces. Calligraphy using texts from the Koran can be seen on simple bowls, as in *case 6,* or on richly decorated tiles from a tomb in *case 2*, both from Iran.

*Take the North stairs or lift to see Korean pottery (**67**) and Japanese (**92–94** reopening June 2006) .*

Camel from the tomb of the general Liu Tingxun who died in 728 AD (Tang dynasty). The tomb also contained horses, grooms and Buddhist guardian figures in the same combination of colours. (**33**)

Basin from Iznik, Turkey (c.1550), combining abstract motifs with naturalistic treatment of flowers. It may have been used in an Ottoman palace for washing feet. (**34**)

Korean white porcelain 'Full-Moon' jar, Choson dynasty (1392–1910). (**67**)

The pottery traditions of Korea and Japan also reflect strong Chinese influence. In **67** (Korea) the tones of jade-like green and especially white appeal to more austere Confucian taste, as in the 'Full Moon' jar in *case 14*. This pot belonged to two famous 20th-century Western potters, both admirers of Asian ceramics: Bernard Leach and Lucie Rie.

Greece and Rome

Return to the Great Court and take the West door through **4 to 11.**

On the Main floor starting in **12** you can see the development of Mediterranean pottery: boldly decorated pots from Crete in **12**; geometric, black- and then red-figure painted pots from Athens and elsewhere in **13**, **15** and **20**. The black-figured Exekias vase (540–530 BC), found in Italy, is signed by him. It is one of the finest of all Greek vases. It shows Penthesilea, queen of the Amazons, being killed by the Greek hero Achilles during the Trojan wars. It depicts the moment when (according to legend) their eyes met and they fell in love – but too late.

The red-figured vase showing Odysseus and the sirens (480–470 BC) is in **69** *(Upper floor, case 25)*. Odysseus and his crew sail past the island of the sirens; he is strapped to the mast to hear their song; the ears of his crew are plugged with wax so

left
Black-figured Greek wine jar by the painter Exekias (540–530 BC). (**13**)

right
Red-figured Greek wine jar showing Odysseus and the sirens. (480–470 BC). (**69**)

that they can ignore it. Room **69** also has pots given as prizes (originally full of olive oil) in the Greek games at Athens and Olympia. On the Upper floor are terracottas such as the Etruscan sarcophagus in **71**, and many regional styles of pottery in **70–73**.

Europe
Go via 69, 68 and 41 to 42 (Medieval).

Medieval pots and tiles are in **42–43**. Rooms **46–47** trace the development of European ceramics from the Renaissance to the 19th century. Moorish pottery from Spain was highly prized by patrons like the Medici. Their arms are on this vase made at Valencia 1465–75, in **46** *(case 1)*. This is tin-glazed earthenware, with a lustre (a thin coat of silver or copper) applied to an already fired glaze. It is a complex process originating in Iraq, and prone to failure. Italian maiolica, developed from these Islamic sources *(cases 2 and 4)*, is decorated with a range of classical and contemporary subjects. Medici potters attempted to make porcelain, as did the Englishman John Dwight *(case 9)*. His bust of Prince Rupert, nephew of Charles I, is in stoneware *(see p.54)*. This is a process, first developed in 14th-century Rhineland, of firing to a temperature of over 1200°C, providing an extremely hard and impervious vessel.

Lustred vase from Valencia, Spain (1465–75), with the Medici arms. **(46)**

Dutch potters at Delft *(case 10)* imitated the blue and white decoration of Chinese porcelain *(see case 15)*, but not its fine, thin, translucent body. That breakthrough – the first real Western porcelain – came at Meissen in c.1708. Meissen and Italian porcelain is in *case 16*. By the 1740s porcelain was being produced in England: works from the factories at Chelsea, Bow, Lambeth and Worcester are in *cases 17, 20–21.* The richly decorated 'Cleopatra' vases, made at Chelsea, are in *case 18.*

Josiah Wedgwood (1730–95) in Staffordshire not only produced ceramics for patrons such as the Empress Catherine the Great of Russia, British royalty and aristocracy, but also cheaper, mass-produced 'china' for a humbler domestic market. *Case 20* in **46** and *cases 1–2* in **47** show some of this range, including the copy of the Portland Vase (the glass original is in **70**) and the 'Pegasus Vase' he presented to the Museum. Its design was taken by Flaxman from a Greek vase also now in the Museum. The 19th- and 20th-century ceramics in **47** and **48** include pieces inspired by Japan and China as well as plates from Soviet Russia.

Africa *(25)* *Lower floor*
*From the Great Court take the stairs from **24** or the lifts adjacent to the bookshop. Turn left through the sections on wood and metal.*

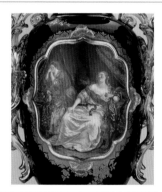

left
Detail from a 'Cleopatra' vase, Chelsea porcelain (1762). (**47**)

right
The 'Pegasus Vase' in pale blue jasperware, made and presented by Josiah Wedgwood (1786). (**47**)

In Africa pots are usually hand made by women although the potter's wheel is used in North African towns. Though cheap and functional, African pots combine absolute utility with great formal beauty and are used even when industrially mass-produced vessels are available. Pots can also have a spiritual symbolism and may contain the spirits of ancestors, deities or even diseases. Marriage often involves making new pots while old pots are smashed when someone dies.

The big pots in the centre of the display show varied decoration. One with multiple spouts is for Ugandan elders to drink beer together through a straw from each spout. On the long wall case are pots for Zulu beer and Algerian oil, and three Ugandan pots burnished to resemble calabashes, made for the royal palace. In *case 22* are pots for use at Asante funerals as grave markers, including a modern Tunisian piece by Khaled Ben Slimane, who also trained in Japan and Spain. In *case 20* are two water pots: an elegant Moroccan one decorated with a black resin pattern, and a Nigerian jar. The red slip applied to its body prevents leakage while the grooves around the neck increase evaporation for cooling and provide a good grip. The round bottom allows it to be set down at any angle and it fits comfortably inside a head ring to be carried.

Ugandan pots (19th–20th century) made for the Baganda king's palace. (**25**)

Sculpture

You might begin in the Great Court by looking at the range of sculptures shown there and then decide which zones of the Museum to visit. You will need to imagine the missing colour and the often splendid context from which these sculptures came: temples, palaces and tombs.

Ancient rulers are commemorated throughout the Museum, usually with a stylised image rather than what we would call a portrait. Here by the West door to **4** are two heads of the Egyptian Pharaoh Amenhotep III (c.1400 BC) from a pair of colossal statues by his tomb at Thebes (modern Luxor). The Assyrian stela that presides over the West café is of King Ashurnasirpal II (884–859 BC) from Nimrud in Iraq, with a cuneiform account of his achievements.

To see more monumental sculpture go into **4** *(Egypt)* and **6–10** *(Ancient Near East)*. Giant, human-headed, winged creatures in pairs guarded Assyrian palace entrances in the 9th to 7th centuries BC (**10**).

above
Roman statue of a youth on horseback (2nd century AD).
(**Great Court**)

right
Human-headed winged bull from Khorsabad, Assyria (c.710 BC), one of six gateway figures in the Museum. This has five legs so that it can be viewed from the front or side. (**10**)

Assyrian palace friezes operate on very different principles from later Greek temple friezes – such as those of the Parthenon. The lion hunts (**10**) are especially worth seeing, as is the Assyrian siege of Lachish in 701 BC. An inscription hails the victorious Sennacherib as 'king of the universe' (**10**). Archaeology has revealed evidence of the siege engines and ramps depicted on the frieze.

Greek and Roman sculpture in the Great Court reflects the monumental age of the Seven Wonders of the Ancient World. The massive marble lion of the late 4th century BC *(see p.44)*, from Knidos (southwest Turkey), crowned a huge tomb. Its hollow eyes were probably inset with

glass to catch the light. The mounted Roman on horseback (2nd century AD, restored during the 16th century, probably with a different head) shows how Roman art evolved from late Greek or Hellenistic art (**22**). To trace this development, go through the West door via **4** *(turn left and then right at the end)* into **11** *(Cycladic art)* and follow the evolution of the human figure in **13–15**, **17** *(Nereid Monument)*, **18** *(Parthenon)* and **19–23**, culminating with Roman marble versions of lost Greek originals.

*You can see more Roman sculpture in **83–85**, Lower floor and in **70** and **49**, Upper floor.*

Cycladic figurine. (**11**)

Caryatid from the Porch of the Maidens on the Erechtheion in Athens (late 5th century BC). (**19**)

left
Roman marble greyhounds (1st–2nd century AD), part of the Townley Collection. (**84**)

right
Roman marble copy of a 5th-century BC Greek bronze of a discus thrower, from Hadrian's Villa, Tivoli. (**South stairs**)

Easter Island statue
(11th–17th century).
(24)

Other sculpture in the Great Court area indicates Asia. Two Chinese figures guard the North door from the Great Court as they once guarded a spirit road leading to a 17th-century tomb. They have Korean features and carry Korean-style boxes.

Go through the North door into the Wellcome Trust Gallery **(24)** to see the Easter Island statue from the Pacific world, excavated from a sacred house in Rapanui in 1868. It would have originally fulfilled its sacred role on a platform near the sea on the west side of the island.

Rapanui was first sighted by Europeans on Easter Day in 1722, and was later visited by Captain Cook. The islanders carved this statue from basalt after c.1000 AD. Later, probably around the 1550s, images relating to the birdman cult were carved onto its back. The island now belongs to Chile, 2,300 miles to the east. Cook and other explorers in the Pacific are featured in the Enlightenment Gallery **(1)** *(East door)*, as is the collecting of sculpture.

Return to the Great Court, go through the North door and through **24** *to the North stairs and the giant Chinese figure of the Amitabha Buddha (585 AD).* By this time Buddhism was

left
Seated figure of the Buddha (5th–6th century AD). **(33)**

right
Chinese marble figure of the Buddha Amitabha (585 AD), 5 metres high. **(North stairs)**

establishing itself with state and individual patronage. This statue is not of the founder of Buddhism, but of the Buddha who presides over the Western Paradise. The missing hands probably expressed fearlessness and granting a wish.

In the adjacent Hotung Gallery (**33**), at the far right-hand end, is a Chinese painting showing three Bodhisattvas presiding over the Western Paradise. Other Buddhist figures are on stylised lotus bases

(a symbol of divinity and purity), with similar hand gestures (mudras).

A particularly expressive example is the gilt and bronze Tara from Sri Lanka to the left. At the far left-hand end are sculptures from the Buddhist stupa at Amaravati in southeast India (1st century BC–3rd century AD). A major Buddhist stupa (shrine) usually housed a holy relic; its dome-shaped exterior was often decorated with sculpture to be seen by pilgrims as they processed around it.

Hindu sculptures in **33** depict key figures such as Ganesh *(see p.32)*, Shiva and Parvati, and the various forms of Vishnu, best known today as Rama or Krishna.

Drum slab from the Buddhist shrine at Amaravati, India (2nd–3rd century AD). (**33a**)

left
Gilt bronze figure of Tara from Sri Lanka (8th century AD). (**33**)

right
Bronze figure of Shiva Nataraja (c.1100 AD). (**33**)

Native North American
mask from the
Northwest Coast. (**26**)

*On your return to the Great Court
to see Mexican sculpture (27),
turn left in the Wellcome Trust
Gallery (24) and then through 26.*

There is a great variety of type,
date and style of sculpture in the
Mexican Gallery. In the centre
are two-dimensional figures of
deities from the Huaxtec culture
(900–1450 AD). The fertility
goddess with elaborate head-
dress touches her womb;
offerings were made to her (as
to other deities here) to secure
human and agricultural fertility.
Smaller Olmec pieces *(by the far
door)* reflect the monumental
style of colossal heads from
1200–400 BC. Maya culture
encompassed eastern Mexico,
Belize, Guatemala and part of

Honduras. The Maya lintels
(c.725 AD) from the temple at
Yaxchilan depict significant
moments in the life of the ruler
of Yaxchilan, Lord Shield Jaguar,
and his principal wife Lady Xoc.
A jade plaque in the same
expressive style, showing in
detail a wealth of costume and
jewellery, depicts a seated Maya
king with a palace dwarf. It
comes from the great site at
Teotihuacan.

The Aztec fire serpent in the
centre of the gallery is presented
as a jagged bolt of lightning from
the sky; the rattlesnake is a
precise depiction down to its
fangs and split tongue. Other
sculptures are of feathered
snake deities, double-headed
serpents, and skulls, inlaid with

left
Limestone Maya Lintel 16
from Yaxchilan ('Place of
the Split Sky'), Mexico
(c.755–70 AD). (**27**)

right
Nkisi figure from the
Democratic Republic of
Congo (c.1900). (**25**)

turquoise, shell and pearl, or carved in stone.

A North American totem pole by the East stairs is next door. It comes from a 19th-century Haida settlement in Northwest Canada, and tells the story of the Raven, creator of all things, stealing fish from a village at the bottom of the ocean, and also of an exiled young man with supernatural powers who hides in a whale that is then washed up at his home village.

The range of African sculpture in **25** *(Lower floor)* is extraordinary: from contemporary work in metal by Sokari Douglas Camp to bronzes, ivories, and wooden masks and figures. African sculpture inspired artists such as Picasso and Henry Moore (to whom these galleries are dedicated).

Moore later recalled the impact that art from Africa, Mexico and Egypt had made on him as an art student. Of these Azande figures he wrote: 'What a remarkably inventive interpretation of arms, shoulders, elbows and fingers. To discover, as a young student, that the African carvers could interpret the human figure to this degree but still keep and intensify the expression, encouraged me to be more adventurous and experimental.'

left
Wooden figure of the 17th-century founder of the Kuba dynasty with a mancala game-board (c.18th century), from the Democratic Republic of Congo. (**25**)

right
Azande male and female wooden figures, southern Sudan (19th–20th century). (**25**)

The Seven Wonders of the Ancient World

The list of the Seven Wonders varies.
That most generally accepted today includes
the pyramids of Egypt, the colossus of
Rhodes, the hanging gardens of Babylon, the
temple of Artemis (Diana) at Ephesos, the
Mausoleum at Halikarnassos, the lighthouse
at Alexandria and the statue of Zeus at
Olympia by Pheidias. The walls of Babylon
sometimes appear on the list.

Parts of two of the Wonders are in the Museum: the Mausoleum at Halikarnassos (modern Bodrum in Turkey) and the temple of Artemis at Ephesos (also Turkey). Sculpture from the Mausoleum is in **21**. Maussollos was a 4th-century BC ruler of Karia, which was under Greek cultural influence – hence the Greek-style sculptures. It had become part of the Persian empire but with local rulers. His monument at Halikarnassos has given us the word for other elaborate tombs since; it collapsed in the 13th century, probably after an earthquake, and its stone was re-used. The Mausoleum consisted of a stepped colonnade of 36 columns. Above this was a pyramid of 24 steps surmounted by a four-horse chariot. The

left
Colossal statue once thought to be Maussollos, ruler of Karia, from the Mausoleum at Halikarnassos (mid-4th century BC). (**21**)

right
Marble column drum from the temple of Artemis at Ephesos (c.325–300 BC). (**22**)

monument was probably covered with other sculptures: statues of lions at the base of the pyramid and perhaps 36 colossal portraits between the columns. There was room for further statues on the middle step and 88 life-sized figures at the base. The sculptures now in the Museum include two colossal statues, once thought to be Maussollos and Artemisia (his sister and his wife), but more probably members of the ruling dynasty of Karia.

A marble column drum from the temple of Artemis at Ephesos is in the Hellenistic Room (**22**), next door to the Mausoleum Room. Carved on the column drum are a seated man (Pluto) and a standing woman (Persephone), gods of the underworld. They appear to be

watching the preparations for departure made by a woman who stands muffled in a heavy mantle, a fold of which she draws out from her shoulder in a gesture often made by brides. Beckoning her from her right is a youthful winged figure, whose sword suggests that he is Thanatos, Death; on her other side stands Hermes, the guide of the dead. The doomed woman may be Iphigenia, sacrificed by the Greeks to Artemis (the goddess of the temple) to win a fair wind for their passage to Troy. The column drum dates from c.325–300 BC and comes from the building which replaced the temple destroyed in 356 BC. The site at Ephesos is also featured in **82** (*Lower floor*) and **70** (*Rome, Upper floor*).

Horse with a bronze bridle from the Mausoleum. (**21**)

SEE ALSO

Material related to other Wonders can be found as follows:

- Statue of Zeus at Olympia (**69**)
- Pyramids of Egypt (**64**)
- Hanging Gardens of Babylon are assumed to be from the time of Nebuchadnezzar II, c.600 BC (**55–56**). See also the royal gardens depicted in **88–89**, *Lower floor*

Further reading

The Seven Wonders of the Ancient World, ed. P. Clayton and M. Price, London, 1988 (reprinted 1993).

The Seven Wonders of the Ancient World, Diana Bentley, British Museum Press, 2001, is a well-illustrated account for families and younger readers.

Time

There is evidence for the measurement of time from many cultures. The Museum's largest collection is of European clocks and watches in **44** *(Upper floor)*. First look at the astrolabes in **42** *(case 12)*, an example of how medieval Europe learnt from the Islamic world. By computing the position of the sun and stars, they helped to calculate the time of day and night. Islamic astrolabes are also in **34** and **1**.

In **44** start with *section 1* (medieval), with a weight-driven 'frame' clock like that from Cassiobury Park, Hertfordshire. This clock was probably designed to be wound every 24 hours and to tell the time on a large dial on the exterior of the building. No domestic clocks from before

1400 survive, but one from c.1450 can be seen in *section 3*, far corner. The earliest mechanical clocks probably struck a single stroke on the bell at the hour, just as many of the water clocks in the ancient and Islamic worlds did.

While many modest chamber clocks were being made for the rich, a few immensely elaborate clocks were designed for Renaissance courts. One of the finest is the magnificent carillon clock of Isaac Habrecht made in 1589. It is a version of the great astronomical clock in Strasburg Cathedral by the same maker. One of the most imaginative of the surviving 'toys' is the large nef (or ship) made at Augsburg, c.1585. The striking of the hours and

Astrolabe from Iran (1712). Part of Sir Hans Sloane's founding bequest, now displayed in the Enlightenment Gallery. (**1**)

the quarters was performed by sailors standing in the two crows' nests on the main mast. The ship was mounted on a wheeled carriage so that it could move along a table, propelled by clockwork, which simultaneously caused its cannon to be fired. The ship pitched up and down, as if at sea. A fanfare started up as the Heralds and the Electors of the Holy Roman Empire processed before the Emperor, who moved his head and the hand that holds the sceptre.

Behind are displays of watches from the 16th century onwards in exquisite gilded and enamelled cases. On the other side of the gallery in *section 8* are major 17th-century clocks, notably by the Englishman Thomas Tompion. His royal clock of 1689, with the silver figure of Britannia, is the first pendulum-controlled spring-driven clock to go for one full year without rewinding. The Italian night-clock by Campani (Rome, 1683) was designed to be read in the dark from a distance and is almost entirely silent.

The 18th-century precision timepieces, by Harrison, Mudge and Arnold, were for use at sea in order to define location precisely, at a time when ships could be easily wrecked through faulty navigation.

Finally, look at the 'clock with ball rolling down an incline plane' made in 1810, another attempt to produce a perfect timekeeper.

German ship clock made in Augsburg, c.1585. One of the spectacular automaton clocks of the Renaissance. (**44**)

Royal clock of 1689, British, made by the great clockmaker Thomas Tompion for the bedchamber of King William III and Queen Mary at Kensington Palace. (**44**)

Writing

The British Museum is one of the best places to trace the development of writing worldwide. Many of the cultures reflected in the Museum did not have writing. Today we can appreciate their complex organisation, beliefs and technologies by close attention to archaeological evidence, continuing traditions and the written commentary of others (not always very reliable).

*Take the Great Court stairs to the Upper floor (lifts available) and go over the bridge to **56**.*

Ancient Near East

Starting with *cases 3 and 4* you can follow the origins of writing from before 3000 BC in Sumer (ancient Iraq). Writing on wet clay tablets with a wedge-shaped tool is called cuneiform after the Latin word for wedge. It was last used c.75 AD. Previous systems of symbols from Uruk in Sumer are shown alongside early temple receipts in cuneiform listing sacks of grain and heads of cattle. In the other half of the gallery *(case 18)* are cylinder seals and writing from c.2400 BC, as well as hymns, accounts of omens, medical models and mathematical

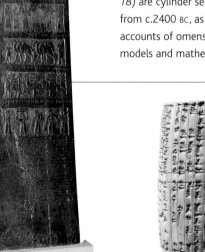

left
The Black Obelisk showing tribute brought to the Assyrian king (late 9th century BC). (**6**)

right
Babylonian cylinder of Nabonidus, with inscription mentioning Belshazzar (6th century BC). (**55**)

calculations. In **55** next door is a Babylonian account of the Flood *(case 10)* from 1635 BC; a very early map on a clay tablet from Babylon *(case 15);* and evidence of the Babylonian kings Nebuchadnezzar *(case 16)* and Nabonidus *(case 12),* the latter on a cylinder recording the restoration of the sun god's temple.

On the Main floor evidence of cuneiform in **6–10** includes the Black Obelisk (**6**), late 9th century BC, showing tribute brought to the Assyrian king.

Ancient Egypt
*From **55** go through **56–59** and right into **61** (closing late 2006).*

In ancient Egypt the earliest hieroglyphs (literally 'sacred writing') appear c.3400 BC, although they were in use before that. They continued without major changes till 390 AD. Flattened stems from the papyrus plant were laid criss-cross in strips and then pasted into rolls. Scribes laid the papyrus on a board and wrote on it with a sharpened reed. Black ink was made from soot, water and a fixative; red ink (for the names of gods and for headings) from red ochre.

The wallcases in **61** are devoted to hieroglyphs, hieratic ('priestly writing') and their decipherment. You will find many examples of hieroglyphs on mummies and coffins in **62–63**, and very early examples from c.3000 BC onward in **64**, Early Egypt *(case 7).*

The Rosetta Stone is on the Main floor. Found by Napoleon's armies in 1799, it was deciphered by Champollion (d.1832). (**4**)

Satirical Egyptian papyrus with animals behaving like humans (c.1200 BC). (**61**, *case 12*)

*At this point you can either return to the front of the Museum, via the Greek and Roman galleries (see box opposite), or go on to look at writing in Asia. From either **61** or **64** go via **66** downstairs to the Hotung Gallery (**33**) and to case 37 at the far right-hand end.*

Asia

In China the first writing also appears c.2000 BC. Animal bones were used as oracles: a question was written on the bone, and the way the bone cracked when exposed to heat was supposed to give the answer *(case 37)*. Later codified and systematised, the Chinese language has continued essentially unchanged from early versions until today. In that respect it is unlike all the other ancient writing systems you will see in the Museum. Chinese paper from the 1st century BC predates European paper (in Spain) by 1,000 years; Chinese printing also predated European by centuries (the earliest dated Chinese printed book, from 868 AD, is now in the British Library).

Calligraphy with ink and brush remains one of the most highly regarded arts throughout East Asia – the Museum collects contemporary calligraphy from China, Japan and Korea, which is often included in changing displays in these galleries.

In South Asia the Indus Valley civilisation (c.2500 BC in modern northwest India and

Enamelled glass mosque lamp from Egypt or Syria, 14th century. (**34**)

opposite
The Franks Casket, whalebone (8th century AD). (**41**)

Pakistan) had a writing system (*33, case 3*) that still awaits decipherment, as do others from Easter Island and Crete, for example.

Arabic developed from c.500 AD, and can be seen in the Addis Gallery (*34, on the floor below 33*) on a Koran and on dishes, boxes, mosque lamps, tiles and coins.

Today the majority of the world uses an alphabet system, which replaced as many as 600 or more symbols (in one version of cuneiform) with about 25. Most languages are still not written down, however, and many are in danger of disappearing.

GREECE, ROME – AND RUNES

From **61** go across the landing to **73–70** and then **69**, Greek and Roman Life. *Case 7* features reading and writing, with much of the evidence from Egypt, because of the hot dry conditions there. Over 100,000 fragments of papyrus have come from the site at Oxyrhynchus, a Greek city 200 miles south of Cairo.

The alphabet was introduced c.750 BC into Greece by the Phoenicians, who were based in modern Lebanon and Syria and had colonies in Carthage (Tunisia), Spain and Sardinia. The Greeks in turn introduced the alphabet to the Etruscans and Romans.

Further extraordinary evidence of Roman writing comes from Roman Britain. There are fragile tablets with writing from Vindolanda on Hadrian's Wall – shopping lists for feasts, and perhaps the earliest piece of women's handwriting in a postscript to an invitation to a birthday party.

In the Early Medieval Room (**41**) is the Franks Casket, with its inscription in runes and Latin, and a mixture of pagan and Christian subjects. The Magi are labelled in runes as they offer Christ their presents.

Further reading
Reading the Past series

The Enlightenment Gallery (1)

Enlightenment: Discovering the World in the 18th Century is a
permanent exhibition in the restored former King's Library. It provides a
new understanding of the Enlightenment in Britain and also acts as an
introduction to the British Museum.

The King's Library formerly housed the library of George III – now
transferred to the British Library in St Pancras – and is the earliest part
of the present Museum building. Constructed in the 1820s, it remains the
finest and largest neo-classical interior in London. The exhibition focuses
on the Enlightenment in Britain during the 18th and early 19th centuries,
the great age of discovery and learning into which the Museum was born
in 1753. The pioneering studies of nature and of man during this period are
the foundations of our modern understanding of the world. The foundation
of the Museum was a characteristic act of the Enlightenment, intended not
only to satisfy the desire of the 'curious' but also 'for the improvement,
knowledge and information of all persons and for the good of the nation'.

On display are nearly 5,000 objects from the reserve collections of
the Museum, with generous loans from the institutions that later sprang
from it: the Natural History Museum and the British Library. The gallery
also features loans, such as George III's scientific instruments from the
Science Museum, and from other collections, including a long-term loan
from the House of Commons Library.

The Act of Parliament which formed the Museum acknowledged that
all arts and sciences were connected. 'Natural and artificial (man-made)
rarities' of the type that filled the Museum are displayed in the original
cases and bookshelves of the King's Library. They evoke the atmosphere of
Montagu House, the Museum's original home, and allow us to compare
different cultures and artefacts in a way that reflects an eighteenth-century
point of view, instead of separating them into individual cultures of the
world as they are displayed in the rest of the Museum today. By exploring
the 'world of nature' and the 'world of man' as they were understood by
men and women of the Enlightenment, we are better equipped to
understand our own world today.

The room is graced by classical sculptures collected by Grand Tourists
and busts of Enlightenment luminaries and collectors. The magnificent

Roman bust of 'Clytie',
c.30 AD. (1)

The King's Library (1823–7), designed by Sir Robert Smirke, has been restored as the Enlightenment Gallery. (1)

Piranesi vase forms a striking centrepiece. The sculpture helps to distinguish the following seven sections of the gallery which explore themes central to the Enlightenment and to the British Museum:

The Natural World: The study and classification of plants, animals, fossils and minerals by such men as Sir Hans Sloane, the botanist Linnaeus and great travellers like Captain Cook and Sir Joseph Banks led to the discovery of new species, the development of modern disciplines such as palaeontology, and a new understanding of the age of the earth.

The Birth of Archaeology: Collections formed by virtuosi and antiquaries, and their study of ancient texts, coins and monuments, led to the birth of modern archaeology and discoveries about the age and origin of man.

Art and Civilisation: Enlightenment approaches to ancient art charted the 'progress' of Western art and civilisation, saw the arrival in the Museum of many of its greatest treasures, and inspired the Classical revival, echoed in Josiah Wedgwood's ceramics.

Classifying the World: Private cabinets of curiosities with their mummies and mermaids, coins and gems, gradually evolved into the modern museum as classification systems developed to organise these 'artificial rarities'. Some of these taxonomies are still in use today.

Ancient Scripts: Throughout the 18th century the transcription, decipherment and translation of ancient and modern hieroglyphs and scripts, especially the Rosetta Stone, opened up the ancient worlds of Egypt, Persia, India, the Far East and even Britain.

Religion, Rites and Magic: British scholars and travellers recorded and studied modern and ancient religions around the world in order to search for common origins and increase their understanding of other cultures.

Trade and Discovery: Employees of trading companies and explorers such as Captain Cook, Sir Joseph Banks and George Vancouver brought back fascinating objects from all over the world which inspired the foundations of modern ethnography.

Wedgwood portrait plaque of Captain James Cook. (1)

Living and dying (24)

Living and dying: Wellcome Trust Gallery opens with an exhibition exploring the different ways in which people around the world seek well-being for themselves and their communities in the face of illness and suffering. This exhibition is about challenges we all share, but to which there are many different responses.

Some societies and some belief systems see well-being in terms of the individual and the human body. Other people think of well-being at the level of the community, as dependent on the maintenance of important relationships. In most societies there are a range of culturally acceptable ways an individual can seek to avert harm and identify its causes and treatments.

The gallery's themes are illustrated with four central presentations: from the Pacific Islands, North America, the Nicobar Islands in the Bay of Bengal, and the Andes. These large-scale cases show some of the ways communities ensure well-being by engaging in relationships with other people (Pacific), animals (Native North America), spirits (Nicobar Islands) and the earth (Andes). Material from many parts of the globe features in two further sections. 'Life's Ordinary Dangers' and 'Your Life in their Hands' illustrate how individuals can protect what they need and those they care for, and seek help in response to sickness and trouble, with objects from the Middle East, Australia, Solomon Islands, Mexico, Asia, Africa and Europe.

Wooden board from Gulf Province, Papua New Guinea (early 20th century). The carving depicts a bush spirit, for which the board may also provide a home. (**24**)

Gold pectoral of the Popayán culture from Colombia (1100–1500). These chest ornaments were worn by priests and shamans to proclaim their powers of access to the hidden, creative sources of life. (**24**)

Painted wooden dancer's mask depicting the Serpent Demon, from Sri Lanka (19th century). (**24**)

'Cradle to Grave', an art installation specially commissioned from Susie Freeman, Liz Lee and David Critchley (Pharmacopoeia), explores biomedical responses to protection and treatment in modern Britain. Images and graphics illustrate some of life's difficulties – trouble, sorrow, need and sickness.

The exhibits range from ancient gold from Central and South America to contemporary collections from Tanzania. 'The Atomic Apocalypse', a vast papier-mâché sculpture from the Mexican Day of the Dead festival, hangs from the ceiling of the gallery. The basalt Easter Island figure known as Hoa Hakananai'a is on open display as is a Haida wooden totem pole from the Northwest Coast of North America, along with other monumental sculptures.

Basalt sculpture known as Hoa Hakananai'a from Easter Island in the South Pacific. Representing an ancestral figure, it was probably first displayed out of doors on a ceremonial platform c.1000, and was later removed to a ritual house. It was collected in 1868 and came into the Museum as a gift of Queen Victoria. (**24**)

Glossary

amphora
A jar with two handles used for transporting or storing liquids, especially wine.

cameo
A hardstone or gem into which a design is cut in relief.

cartonnage
Layers of linen and plaster.

cartoon
A drawing of the principal forms of a composition made to the same scale as the painting or fresco for which it is preparatory.

cloison
A cell formed of thin strips of metal soldered to a metal base, designed to hold the inlay of stone, glass or other material.

drypoint
Printmaking technique whereby a sharp needle is used to work a design on a metal plate.

earthenware
Opaque and coarse ceramic body which is not fully vitrified and remains porous, requiring glazing to make it impervious to liquids.

enamel
A colour consisting of a pigment derived from a metal oxide and a glass flux which is painted over a pre-fired glaze and then fired at a low temperature.

engraving
Print made with a graver, a small metal rod with a sharpened point, pushed across the plate or block.

etching
Print in which the lines incised into a metal plate are bitten by acid.

faience
French term for tin-glazed earthenware (Renaissance and later). Also a glazed ceramic, composed of crushed quartz, which is common in the ancient Near East and Mediterranean.

filigree
A decorative pattern made of wires, sometimes soldered to a background, but often left as openwork.

firing
Process of exposing a clay body to intense heat, initially to harden the clay and then to melt the applied glaze.

glaze
Glassy coating fused to a ceramic body to seal it against moisture and/or to decorate it.

Hellenistic
Greek influences on art and culture particularly under Alexander the Great.

hieratic
A form of Egyptian hieroglyph written with brush pen on papyrus.

hieroglyph
The earliest Egyptian script, in use from c.3000 BC to the 4th century AD.

icon
A Christian painted image of sacred figures or stories.

kouros
A standing naked male in early Greek sculpture.

krater
A wide-mouthed bowl for mixing wine and water.

kylix
A shallow drinking cup with two handles often on a tall stem.

lacquer
A waterproof varnish derived from the sap of a tree, which hardens when exposed to air – the first plastic.

lapis lazuli
A semi-precious blue coloured stone.

lekythos
An oil or perfume bottle.

lithography
Printmaking technique of drawing a design in wax crayon onto a lith or stone.

lustre
Iridescent decoration on ceramic, achieved by depositing a metallic film onto glazes.

maiolica
Italian tin-glazed earthenware.

metope
The square space on a frieze between two dividers (triglyphs).

natron
Naturally occurring salt compound, used to dry the body during mummification.

niello
A black compound of silver, lead, copper and sulphur.

obverse
Front of a coin or medal.

pectoral
Amulet worn on the chest.

pediment
A triangular space formed by the gables above a portico.

porcelain
A white vitreous and translucent ceramic. Translucent porcelain was first made in China, c.10th century AD. In Europe soft-paste porcelain, a glassy substance, was first made in 16th-century Florence. 'True' or hard-paste porcelain, similar to the oriental type, appeared in Saxony c.1708, but was not made in England until more than 60 years later. Bone china, a type of 'artificial' porcelain containing calcined ox bones, was made in England from the end of the 18th century, and became the foundation of the modern English tableware industry.

pyxis
A cylindrical box with a lid, used for cosmetics and jewellery.

recto
The front or more fully worked face of a sheet drawn on both sides. Opposite of verso.

repoussé
Relief decoration on metal, hammered from the underside.

reverse
Back of a coin or medal.

runes
An angular script for carving on wood, stone or ivory by early medieval Germanic peoples.

scarab
Amulet representing the sacred beetle, symbol of the sun-god (Egypt).

stoneware
Dense, non-porous pottery, typically firing to a grey colour at temperatures in excess of 1100°C.

stucco
Plasterwork.

terracotta
Low-fired earthenware, usually red and unglazed.

torc
Gold or silver neck ornament, especially worn by the Celts.

verso
Opposite of recto.

watercolour
A pigment for which water rather than oil is used as a medium. If gum arabic is added it becomes bodycolour or gouache.

woodcut
A relief technique in printmaking, in which the design is drawn directly on the surface of the block and the lines are left standing clear from it.

ziggurat
A rectangular staged temple mound built by the Sumerians and others to honour their gods.

Further reading

All the following titles are published by the British Museum Press unless otherwise stated.
In each section introductory overviews are given first.

British Museum
History & Collections
The Collections of the British Museum,
  ed. David M. Wilson, 2006
Treasures of the British Museum,
  Marjorie Caygill, 2004
The British Museum: 250 Years, Marjorie Caygill,
  2003
The British Museum A-Z Companion,
  Marjorie Caygill, 2005
The Museum of the Mind, John Mack, 2003
The Story of the British Museum, Marjorie
  Caygill, 2002
The British Museum: A History, David M. Wilson,
  2002
Behind the Scenes at the British Museum,
  ed. Andrew Burnett & John Reeve, 2001
Flowers, ed. Marjorie Caygill, 2006
Little Book of Treasures, 2004
Winter: A British Museum Companion,
  ed. Marjorie Caygill, 2004
World Religions: British Museum Visitor's Guide,
  John Reeve, 2006

Buildings
The Great Court and the British Museum,
  Robert Anderson, 2005
The British Museum Reading Room,
  Marjorie Caygill, 2000
Building the British Museum, Marjorie Caygill &
  Christopher Date, 1999

Africa
Africa: Arts and Cultures, ed. John Mack, 2005
Africa in the World: Past and Present, Ben Burt, 2005
African Designs, Rebecca Jewell, 2004
African Textiles, John Picton & John Mack, 1999
The Art of Benin, Paula Girshick Ben-Amos,
  1995
The Kingdom of Kush, Derek A. Welsby, 2001
Medieval Kingdoms of Nubia, Derek A. Welsby,
  2001
North African Textiles, Christopher Spring &
  Julie Hudson, 1995
Silk in Africa, Christopher Spring & Julie
  Hudson, 2002
Smashing Pots: Feats of Clay from Africa,
  Nigel Barley, 1994

Americas
Central & South America
Ancient Mexico in the British Museum, Colin
  McEwan, 1994
Aztec and Maya Myths, Karl Taube, 2002
Inca Myths, Gary Urton, 1999
Alfred Maudslay and the Maya: A Biography,
  Ian Graham, 2002
Nasca: Eighth Wonder of the World?,
  Anthony F. Aveni, 2000
Textiles from Guatemala, Ann Hecht, 2001
Textiles from Mexico, Chloë Sayer, 2002
Turquoise Mosaics from Mexico, C. McEwan et
  al., 2006
Unknown Amazon, ed. C. McEwan, C. Barreto &
  E. Neves, 2001

North America
First Peoples, First Contacts, J.C.H. King, 1999
Imaging the Arctic, ed. J.C.H. King & H.J. Lidchi, 1998
North American Indian Designs, Eva Wilson, 2000

Ancient Egypt

Ancient Egypt: Art, architecture and history, Francesco Tiradritti, 2004

British Museum Book of Ancient Egypt, ed. Stephen Quirke & Jeffrey Spencer, 2001

British Museum Dictionary of Ancient Egypt, Ian Shaw & Paul Nicholson, 2002

The Ancient Egyptian Book of the Dead, trans. Raymond O. Faulkner & ed. Carol Andrews, 2006

Ancient Egyptian Designs, Eva Wilson, 2005

An Ancient Egyptian Herbal, Lise Manniche, 2006

Ancient Egyptian Medicine, John F. Nunn, 2006

Ancient Egyptian Religion, Stephen Quirke, 1992

The Art of Ancient Egypt, Gay Robins, 2000

The Cat in Ancient Egypt, Jaromir Malek, 2006

Concise Introduction Ancient Egypt, T.G.H. James, 2005

Death and the Afterlife in Ancient Egypt, John Taylor, 2001

Early Egypt, A.J. Spencer, 1993

Egypt, Vivian Davies & Renée Friedman, 1999

Egypt after the Pharaohs, Alan K. Bowman, 1996

Egypt from Alexander to the Copts: An Archaeological and Historical Guide, ed. Roger S. Bagnall & Dominic W. Rathbone, 2004

Egyptian Mummies, Carol Andrews, 2004

Egyptian Myths, George Hart, 2005

Eternal Egypt: Masterworks of Ancient Art from the British Museum, Edna R. Russmann, 2001

Little Book of Mummies, 2004

Magic in Ancient Egypt, Geraldine Pinch, 2006

Masterpieces of Ancient Egypt, Nigel Studwick, 2006

Monuments of Ancient Egypt, Jeremy Stafford-Deitsch, 2001

Mummy: The Inside Story, John Taylor, 2005

The Rosetta Stone, Richard Parkinson, 2005

Sudan: Ancient Treasures, ed. Derek A. Welsby & Julie R. Anderson, 2004

The Tale of Peter Rabbit, hieroglyph edn, 2005

Voices from Ancient Egypt: An Anthology of Middle Kingdom Writings, R.B. Parkinson, 2004

Women in Ancient Egypt, Gay Robins, 2004

Ancient Greece & Rome

British Museum Book of Greek and Roman Art, Lucilla Burn, 2005

Classical Love Poetry, ed. & trans. Jonathan Williams & Clive Cheesman, 2004

Hellenistic Art from Alexander the Great to Augustus, Lucilla Burn, 2004

The Portland Vase, Susan Walker, 2004

Sex or Symbol? Erotic Images of Greece and Rome, Catherine Johns, 2005

The Greek World

Ancient Cyprus, Veronica Tatton-Brown, 1997

Ancient Greece: Art, Architecture and History, Marina Belozerskaya & Kenneth Lapatin, 2005

The Ancient Olympic Games, Judith Swaddling, 2004

Classical Athens, Alexandra Villing, 2005

Cycladic Art, J. Lesley Fitton, 1999

The Elgin Marbles, Brian Cook, 2005

Etruscan Civilization: A Cultural History, Sybille Haynes, 2005

Etruscan Myths, Larissa Bonfante & Judith Swaddling, 2006

The Etruscans: Art, Architecture and History, Federica Borrelli & Maria Cristina Targia, 2004

Greek Architecture and its Sculpture, Ian Jenkins, 2006

Greek Designs, Sue Bird, 2003

Greek Myths, Lucilla Burn, 2004

Greek Vases, Dyfri Williams, 1999

Minoans, J. Lesley Fitton, 2002

The Parthenon Frieze, Ian Jenkins, 2002
Women in Ancient Greece, Sue Blundell, 1995

The Roman World
Ancient Rome: Art, architecture and history,
   Ada Gabucci, 2004
Ancient Mosaics, Roger Ling, 1998
*Gladiators and Caesars: The Power of Spectacle
   in Ancient Rome*, Eckart Kohne & Cornelia
   Ewigleben, 2000
Roman Italy, T.W. Potter, 1992
Roman Myths, Jane F. Gardner, 2005
Roman Designs, Eva Wilson, 1999
The Warren Cup, Dyfri Williams, 2006

The Ancient Near East
Ancient Near Eastern Art, Dominique Collon,
   1995
Ancient Persia, John Curtis, 2006
*Art and Empire: Treasures from Assyria in the
   British Museum*, ed. J.E. Curtis & J.E. Reade,
   2005
Assyrian Sculpture, Julian Reade, 2006
Babylonians, H.W.F. Saggs, 2000
The Bible in the British Museum, T.C. Mitchell, 2006
*British Museum Dictionary of the Ancient Near
   East*, ed. Piotr Bienkowski & Alan Millard, 2000
Canaanites, Jonathan Tubb, 2005
Agatha Christie and Archaeology, ed. Charlotte
   Trumpler, 2003
*Gods, Demons and Symbols of Ancient
   Mesopotamia: An Illustrated Dictionary*,
   Jeremy Black & Anthony Green, 2004
Mesopotamia, Julian Reade, 2005
Mesopotamian Myths, Henrietta McCall, 2004
Forgotten Empire: The World of Ancient Persia,
   ed. John E. Curtis & Nigel Tallis, 2006
Persian Myths, Vesta Sarkhosh Curtis, 2006
The Persian Empire: A History, Lindsay Allen, 2005
Phoenicians, Glenn Markoe, 2002
The Queen of the Night, Dominique Collon, 2005
Roman Syria and the Near East, Kevin Butcher, 2003

Asia
China
British Museum Book of Chinese Art, ed. Jessica
   Rawson, 2000
The Art of Calligraphy in Modern China, Gordon S.
   Barrass, 2002
Chinese (Reading the Past), Oliver Moore, 2000
Chinese Art in Detail, Carol Michaelson & Jane
   Portal, 2006
*Chinese Calligraphy: Standard Script for
   Beginners*, Qu Lei Lei, 2005
Chinese Jade from the Neolithic to the Qing,
   Jessica Rawson, 2002
Chinese Love Poetry, ed. Jane Portal, 2006
Chinese Myths, Anne Birrell, 2000
Chinese Pottery and Porcelain, Shelagh Vainker,
   2005
Chinese Silk: A Cultural History, Shelagh
   Vainker, 2004
*First Masterpiece of Chinese Painting: The
   Admonitions Scroll*, Shane McCausland, 2003
Forbidden City, Frances Wood, 2005
Ming Ceramics in the British Museum, Jessica
   Harrison-Hall, 2001
Painted Buddhas of Xinjiang, Reza et al., 2002
Aurel Stein on the Silk Road, Susan Whitfield,
   2004

Japan
*Japanese Art: Masterpieces in the British
   Museum*, Lawrence Smith, Victor Harris &
   Timothy Clark, 1990
100 Views of Mount Fuji, Timothy Clark, 2001
*Cutting Edge: Japanese Swords in the British
   Museum*, Victor Harris, 2004
Floating World: Japan in the Edo period,
   John Reeve, 2006
Haiku, ed. David Cobb, 2005
Japanese Art in Detail, John Reeve, 2006
*A Japanese Menagerie: Animal Pictures by
   Kawanabe Kyosai*, Rosina Buckland, Timothy
   Clark & Shigeru Oikawa, 2006

Modern Japanese Prints 1912–1989, Lawrence
  Smith, 1994
Shinto: The Sacred Art of Ancient Japan,
  ed. Victor Harris, 2001

Korea
Korea: Art and Archaeology, Jane Portal, 2000

South & South-East Asia
Amaravati: Buddhist Sculpture from the Great
  Stupa, Robert Knox, 1992
Bengali Myths, T. Richard Blurton, 2006
The Buddha, Delia Pemberton, 2004
Burma: Art and Archaeology, ed. Alexandra
  Green & T. Richard Blurton, 2002
Hindu Art, T. Richard Blurton, 2002
Hindu Myths, A.L. Dallapiccola, 2003
Hindu Visions of the Sacred, A.L. Dallapiccola,
  2004
Indian Love Poetry, A.L. Dallapiccola, 2006
Vietnam Behind the Lines: Images from the War
  1965–75, Jessica Harrison-Hall, 2002
Visions from the Golden Land: Burma and the
  Art of Lacquer, Ralph Isaacs & T. Richard
  Blurton, 2000

Britain & Europe
Prehistoric Europe
Britain and the Celtic Iron Age, Simon James &
  Valery Rigby, 1997
Celtic Art, Ian Stead, 2003
Celtic Myths, Miranda Green, 2003
Early Celtic Designs, Ian Stead & Karen Hughes,
  1997
Little Book of Celts, 2004
Women in Prehistory, Margaret Ehrenberg,
  1995

Roman Britain
Roman Britain, T.W. Potter, 2003
Roman Britain (Exploring the Roman World),
  T.W. Potter & Catherine Johns, 2002

The Hoxne Treasure, Roger Bland & Catherine
  Johns, 1994
Life and Letters on the Roman Frontier:
  Vindolanda and its People, Alan K. Bowman,
  2006

Medieval Europe
Byzantium, Rowena Loverance, 2004
Chronicles of the Vikings: Records, Memorials
  and Myths, R.I. Page, 2002
The Decorated Style, Nicola Coldstream, 1999
Early Medieval Designs, Eva Wilson, 1983
English Tilers, Elizabeth Eames, 2004
The Lewis Chessmen, James Robinson, 2005
The Lewis Chessmen and the Enigma of the
  Hoard, Neil Stratford, 1997
Masons and Sculptors, Nicola Coldstream,
  2004
The Medieval Garden, Sylvia Landsberg, 2005
Medieval Love Poetry, ed. John Cherry, 2005
Norse Myths, R.I. Page, 2004
Russian Myths, Elizabeth Warner, 2002
Scribes and Illuminators, Christopher de Hamel,
  2006
The Sutton Hoo Ship Burial, Angela Care Evans,
  2000
Sutton Hoo: Burial Ground of Kings?, Martin
  Carver, 2000

Renaissance & Later Europe
William Blake, Bethan Stevens, 2005
Britain, Lindsay Stainton, 2005
Christ, Rowena Loverance, 2004
Albrecht Dürer and his Legacy, Giulia Bartrum,
  2002
Enlightenment: Discovering the World in the
  18th Century, ed. Kim Sloan, 2005
Ferdinand Columbus: Renaissance Collector,
  Mark P. McDonald, 2005
French Drawings: Clouet to Seurat, Perrin Stein,
  2005
Goya's Prints, Juliet Wilson-Bareau, 1996

London 1753, Sheila O'Connell, 2005
Looking at Prints, Drawings and Watercolours: A Guide to Technical Terms, Paul Goldman, 2006
Medicine Man, Ken Arnold & Danielle Olsen, 2003
Michelangelo, Hugo Chapman, 2006
Michelangelo Drawings: Closer to the Master, Hugo Chapman, 2006
Mrs Delany: Her life and her flowers, Ruth Hayden, 2005
Objects of Virtue: Art in Renaissance Italy, Luke Syson & Dora Thornton, 2004
Old Master Drawings from the Malcolm Collection, Martin Royalton-Kisch, Hugo Chapman & Stephen Coppel, 1996
Samuel Palmer: Vision and Landscape, W. Vaughan et al., 2006
The Print in Italy 1550–1620, Michael Bury, 2001
Prints and Printmaking, Antony Griffiths, 2004
Rembrandt the Printmaker, M. Royalton-Kisch et al., 2000
J.M.W. Turner: Watercolours, Kim Sloan, 1998

Modern Europe
Decorative Arts 1850–1950, Judy Rudoe, 1994
Antony Gormley Drawing, Anna Moszynska, 2002
London, Sheila O'Connell, 2005
Modern Scandinavian Prints, Frances Carey, 1997
The Print in Germany, Frances Carey & Antony Griffiths, 1984
Towards Post-Modernism: Design since 1851, Michael Collins, 1994

Conservation & Scientific Research
The Art of the Conservator, ed. Andrew Oddy, 1992
Earthly Remains: The History and Science of Preserved Human Bodies, Andrew T. Chamberlain & Michael Parker Pearson, 2004

Making Faces: Using Forensic and Archaeological Evidence, John Prag & Richard Neave, 1999
Porcelain Repair and Restoration: A Handbook, Nigel Williams, rev. L. Hogan & M. Bruce-Mitford, 2002
Radiocarbon Dating, Sheridan Bowman, 1990
Science and the Past, ed. Sheridan Bowman, 1991

The Islamic World
Islamic Art, Barbara Brend, 2005
Islamic Art in Detail, Sheila R. Canby, 2006
Islamic Designs, Eva Wilson, 2005
Islamic Metalwork, Rachel Ward, 2000
Islamic Textiles, Patricia L. Baker, 1995
Islamic Tiles, Venetia Porter, 2005
Iznik Pottery, John Carswell, 2006
Mughal Miniatures, J.M. Rogers, 2006
The Golden Age of Persian Art 1501–1722, Sheila R. Canby, 2002
Persian Love Poetry, Vesta Sarkhosh Curtis & Sheila R. Canby, 2006
Persian Painting, Sheila R. Canby, 2004
Word into Art: Artists of the Modern Middle East, Venetia Porter, 2006

Animals
British Museum Book of Cats, Juliet Clutton-Brock, 2005
The Cat in Ancient Egypt, Jaromir Malek, 2006
Cats, ed. Delia Pemberton, 2006
A Japanese Menagerie: Animal Pictures by Kawanabe Kyosai, Rosina Buckland, Timothy Clark & Shigeru Oikawa, 2006
Little Book of Cats, 2004
Horses: History, Myth, Art, Catherine Johns, 2006

Glass
5000 Years of Glass, ed. Hugh Tait, 2000
Gilded and Enamelled Glass from the Middle East, ed. Rachel Ward, 1997

Glass in Britain and Ireland AD 350–1100,
ed. Jennifer Price, 2000
The Portland Vase, Susan Walker, 2004

Jewellery

7000 Years of Jewellery, ed. Hugh Tait, 2006
Ancient Egyptian Jewellery, Carol Andrews,
1996
Ethnic Jewellery, ed. John Mack, 2002
Greek Gold, Dyfri Williams & Jack Ogden, 1995
Treasure: Finding Our Past, Richard Hobbs, 2003

Money and Medals

Money: A History, ed. Catherine Eagleton &
Jonathan Williams, 2006
Badges, Philip Attwood, 2004
*Beauty and the Banknote: Images of Women on
Paper Money*, Virginia Hewitt, 1994

Myths

Aztec and Maya Myths, Karl Taube, 2002
Bengali Myths, T. Richard Blurton, 2006
Celtic Myths, Miranda Green, 2003
Chinese Myths, Anne Birrell, 2000
Egyptian Myths, George Hart, 2005
Etruscan Myths, Larissa Bonfante & Judith
Swaddling, 2006
Greek Myths, Lucilla Burn, 2004
Hindu Myths, A.L. Dallapiccola, 2003
Inca Myths, Gary Urton, 1999
Mesopotamian Myths, Henrietta McCall, 2004
Norse Myths, R.I. Page, 2004
Persian Myths, Vesta Sarkhosh Curtis, 2006
Roman Myths, Jane F. Gardner, 2005
Russian Myths, Elizabeth Warner, 2002
The Story of Bacchus, Andrew Dalby, 2005
The Story of Venus, Andrew Dalby, 2005
World of Myths: Vol. 1, Marina Warner, 2005
World of Myths: Vol. 2, Felipe Fernández-
Armesto, 2004

Pacific World

Easter Island, Jo Anne Van Tilburg, 1994
Hoa Hakananai'a, Jo Anne Van Tilburg, 2004
Maori: Art and Culture, ed. D.C. Starzecka, 1998
Pacific Designs, Rebecca Jewell, 2004
*Pacific Encounters: Art and Divinity in Polynesia
1760–1860*, Steven Hooper, 2006

Pottery

10,000 Years of Pottery, Emmanuel Cooper,
2002
*Blue & White: Chinese Porcelain around the
World*, John Carswell, 2000
Chelsea Porcelain, Elizabeth Adams, 2001
Chinese Pottery and Porcelain, Shelagh Vainker,
2005
French Porcelain, Aileen Dawson, 2000
*German Stoneware 1200–1900: Archaeology
and Cultural History*, David Gaimster, 1997
Greek Vases, Dyfri Williams, 1999
Islamic Tiles, Venetia Porter, 2005
Iznik Pottery, John Carswell, 2006
Ming Ceramics in the British Museum, Jessica
Harrison-Hall, 2001
Pottery in the Making: World Ceramic Traditions,
ed. Ian Freestone & David Gaimster, 1997
Smashing Pots: Feats of Clay from Africa,
Nigel Barley, 1994

Sculpture

Assyrian Sculpture, Julian Reade, 2006
The Elgin Marbles, Brian Cook, 2005
Greek Architecture and its Sculpture, Ian
Jenkins, 2006
Human Image, ed. J.C.H. King, 2000
The Parthenon Frieze, Ian Jenkins, 2002

Textiles

5000 Years of Textiles, ed. Jennifer Harris, 2006
African Textiles, John Picton & John Mack, 1999
The Art of the Loom, Ann Hecht, 2001
Chinese Silk: A Cultural History, Shelagh
    Vainker, 2004
Embroiderers, Kay Staniland, 2006
Embroidery from Afghanistan, Sheila Paine, 2006
Embroidery from India and Pakistan, Sheila Paine, 2001
Embroidery from Palestine, Shelagh Weir, 2006
Indigo, Jenny Balfour-Paul, 1998
Islamic Textiles, Patricia L. Baker, 1995
Miao Textiles from China, Gina Corrigan, 2006
Natural Dyes, Gwen Fereday, 2003
North African Textiles, Christopher Spring &
    Julie Hudson, 1995
Printed and Dyed Textiles from Africa, John
    Gillow, 2001
Silk in Africa, Christopher Spring & Julie
    Hudson, 2002
Textiles from Guatemala, Ann Hecht, 2001
Textiles from Mexico, Chloë Sayer, 2002
Thai Textiles, Susan Conway, 2001

Time

Clocks, David Thompson, 2005
Clocks and Watches, Hugh Tait, 1983
Keeping Time, Richard Good, 1993
Victorian Clocks, Richard Good, 1996

Writing

Reading the Past series
Arabic Calligraphy: Naskh Script for Beginners,
    Mustafa Ja'far, 2006
British Museum Book of Egyptian Hieroglyphs,
    Neil Spencer & Claire Thorne, 2003
Chinese Calligraphy: Standard Script for
    Beginners, Qu Lei Lei, 2005
How to Read Egyptian Hieroglyphs: A step-by-
    step guide to teach yourself, Mark Collier &
    Bill Manley, 2006

For children

African Crafts with step-by-step instructions,
    Lynne Garner, 2005
Ancient Egypt Pop-Up Book, James Putnam,
    2004
The Ancient Greek Olympics, Richard Woff,
    1999
Archaeology: Discovering the Past,
    John Orna-Ornstein, 2002
British Museum Fun Books: Ancient Egypt,
    Ancient Greece, Ancient Rome, Wonders of
    the Ancient World, Sandy Ransford
British Museum Illustrated Atlas of Ancient
    Egypt, Delia Pemberton, 2005
British Museum Encyclopaedia of Native North
    America, Rayna Green with Melanie
    Fernandez, 1999
British Museum Illustrated Encyclopaedia of
    Ancient Egypt, Geraldine Harris & Delia
    Pemberton, 2005
British Museum Illustrated Encyclopaedia of
    Ancient Greece, Sean Sheehan, 2002
British Museum Illustrated Encyclopaedia of
    Ancient Rome, Mike Corbishley, 2003
Egyptian Mummies: People from the past, Delia
    Pemberton, 2000
The Egyptian Queen Beauty Book, Delia
    Pemberton, 2001
Everyday Life in Ancient Egypt, Neil Morris,
    2003
Everyday Life in Ancient Rome, Neil Grant, 2003
Fantastic Mummies, John Taylor, 2004
Games, Irving Finkel, 2005
Gladiator Survival Kit, Mike Corbishley, 2004
The Great Pyramid: An Interactive Book, Roscoe
    Cooper & Carolyn Croll, 2004
My Egyptian Mummy File, 2003
The Mystery of the Egyptian Mummy, Joyce
    Filer, 2003

The Mystery of the Hieroglyphs, Carol Donoughue, 1999

Mythical Beasts of Greece and Rome, John Harris, illus. Calef Brown, 2005

Origami, Steve & Megumi Biddle, 2005

Pocket Dictionary of Ancient Egyptian Animals, Angela McDonald, 2004

Pocket Dictionary of Ancient Egyptian Gods and Goddesses, George Hart, 2005

Pocket Dictionary of Ancient Egyptian Mummies, Nigel Strudwick, 2004

Pocket Dictionary of Greek & Roman Gods & Goddesses, Richard Woff, 2005

Pocket Dictionary of Heroes & Heroines of Ancient Greece, Richard Woff, 2004

Pocket Dictionary of Kings & Queens of Britain, Katharine Hoare, 2006

Pocket Dictionary of Pharaohs & Queens, Marcel Marée, 2005

Pocket Guide to Ancient Egyptian Hieroglyphs, Richard Parkinson, 2004

Quiz Book of the Ancient World, Carolyn Howitt, 2004

The Seven Wonders of the Ancient World, Diana Bentley, 2001

The Story of Medicine, Judy Lindsay, 2003

The Story of Money, John Orna-Ornstein, 1998

Timeline of the Ancient World, Katharine Wiltshire, 2004

Activity Books

The Ancient Egyptians / *The Ancient Greeks* *The Anglo-Saxons* / *The Assyrians* / *The Aztecs* *The Celts* / *Gladiator* / *Mammoth* / *Mummy* *Prehistoric Britain* / *Pyramid* / *The Romans* *Treasure* / *The Vikings* / *Writing*

Colouring Books

Amazing Animals / *The Amazon Rainforest* *Ancient Egypt* / *Ancient Greece* / *Ancient Rome* *The Anglo-Saxons* / *Aztecs* / *Bible Peoples* *Cats* / *The Celts* / *Masks* / *The Middle Ages* *Mosaics* / *Roman Britain* / *Stained Glass* *The Vikings*

Eyewitness Guides

(in association with Dorling Kindersley)

Ancient Egypt, George Hart, 1990

Ancient Greece, Anne Pearson, 1992

Ancient Rome, Simon James, 1990

Bible Lands, Jonathan Tubb, 1994

Money, Joe Cribb, 1990

Mummy, James Putnam, 1993

Pyramid, James Putnam, 1994

Index

Upper floors
Rooms 36–73, 90–94

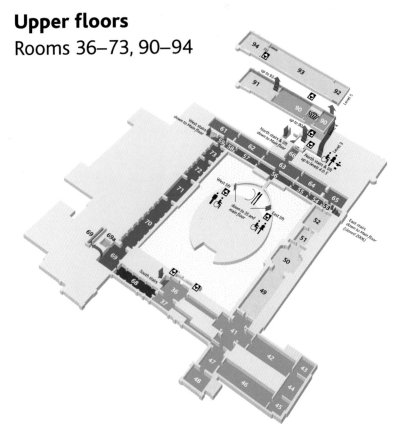